JAMP© & THE RESOLUTION OF THE GLITCH

DR. LAHAB AL-SAMARRAI
CHRISTY FOSTER

Edited by Melissa Mitchell

Published in the United States of America

First Printing Edition, 2022

Table of Contents

JAMP©& The Resolution of the Glitch

ACKNOWLEDGMENTS – DR. LAHAB AL-SAMARRAI

To Sarah – the shining light of my darkness.

ACKNOWLEDGMENTS – CHRISTY FOSTER

I have immense gratitude to those who encouraged me along the way and supported my healing and expansion.

At the end of the day what we really have are relationships and those who love and support us. Trent Foster you are my love, thank you for seeing and encouraging me beyond how I could see myself along the way. You have stood by me during every struggle and success, thank you.

I am so blessed to have my children, now young men Davis and Cole. Thank you for being part of my foundation of love each and every day. You continue to inspire me to become a better person and to enjoy the moments I have with you.

A very special thanks to my dear friend and mentor, Pearl Wagstaff Garff...always known as Miss Pearl. You were a true reflection of love, healing, play, and magic. My life was truly changed when I met you, thank you for showing me what life can be. I continue to inhale all the love you left behind every day of my life.

Boundless gratitude for my sweet mother, Vicki Allsop. I am so blessed to have your unwavering love and courage which you have always given unconditionally. I know I am truly loved, thank you.

ABOUT THE AUTHORS

Dr. Lahab Al-Samarrai

Dr. Lahab Al-Samarrai is a licensed clinical psychotherapist with a Master's in clinical psychology and a Ph.D. in clinical psychotherapy with a sub-specialty in child and adolescent psychotherapy. He has been practicing for over twenty-five years in residential, clinical settings, schools, universities, and private settings. Dr. Lahab has worked extensively with children, adolescents, and adults – providing individual therapy, couples therapy, family therapy, and group therapy as well as lecturing and providing supervision to all student professionals. Dr. Lahab is the past President of the Washington Counseling Association.

Dr. Lahab developed a propriety trauma treatment he named Jungian Advance Motor Processing© (JAMP©) (AL-SAMARRAI, 2020). The IFC's JAMP© (AL-SAMARRAI, 2020) treatment is revolutionary in the treatment of trauma, complex trauma & complex PTSD. His Institute for Conflict has trained and certified 18 JAMP© (AL-SAMARRAI, 2020) Transformational Coaches to date. The Institute For Conflict, & JAMP© (AL-SAMARRAI, 2020) Training Institute with the affiliate Institutions of www.JAMP©University.com, www.JAMP©TrainingInstitute.com, www.JAMP©Online.com & www.instituteforconflict.com are focused on teaching students, practitioners, clinical theory and treatment interventions. The IFC's international conferences, podcasts, courses, and special lectures address successful internal/external conflict transformation and promote researched healing strategies in individuals, schools, hospitals, and companies.

Dr. Lahab has presented at several local & international conferences on clinical psychology, trauma, and on conflict in North America and Western Europe – and has lived in and visited several countries in the Middle East, Europe, and North Africa. He is versatile and bilingual (Arabic and English) and has been studying and exploring psychology, philosophy, political science, and multicultural issues for the past 30 years.

*

Christy Foster

Christy Foster is a Cranio-Sacral therapist and a pioneering educator, speaker, and mentor in the field of Body-Mind Integration. She specializes in teaching Health and Wellness practitioners on how to interpret the subconscious language of the body.

Christy is the first certified teacher of the Psychosomatic Therapy Process in the United States by the Psychosomatic Therapy College, Australia. Her proven system is derived from her 25 years of practical application and education in advanced therapeutic techniques, including CranioSacral Therapy, Emotional Release Trigger Point Therapy, Spinal Touch Therapy, Licensed Massage Therapy, and Energetic-balancing Techniques.

As a teacher, Christy guides practitioners to deeply understand and implement the techniques of BodyMind Integration. Her students learn to systematically decode the two-way communication of the BodyMind. With this integral understanding of how the BodyMind profoundly impacts the physical, mental, and emotional health of every human being, practitioners become healers.

Christy's mission is to empower and create self-awareness for her students and clients. The education she provides serves as a supplement to the expertise of a broad range of Health and Wellness practitioners, therapists, and individuals -- empowering them to

enhance their practices and lives to facilitate more comprehensive and effective therapy.

PREFACE

"The difference between the "natural" individuation process, which runs its course unconsciously, and the one that is consciously realized is tremendous. In the first case, consciousness nowhere intervenes; the end remains as dark as the beginning. In the second case, so much darkness comes to light that the personality is permeated with light and consciousness necessarily gains in scope and insight. The encounter between conscious and unconscious has to ensure that the light that shines in the darkness is not only comprehended by the darkness, but comprehends it."

- Carl Jung

Many of us tend to live our lives through the lens of our past. This, essentially, robs us of the present and prevents us from cultivating our own future. Ultimately, you end up living in a glitch that disempowers you and snuffs your life out before it's even over. That is where JAMP© (AL-SAMARRAI, 2020) comes in.

What is JAMP© (AL-SAMARRAI, 2020)?

JAMP© treatment helps release and integrate splinter images of past conflicts from the complexes where they are stored after they have been dissociated by our natural defense mechanisms. This is accomplished using advanced hypnotic techniques, which help release the image fragments that are held in the complexes.

Once these fragmented images are released, they are understood by the psyche as a symbol and can be integrated. The process in which we interact and receive information with our environment is thus: it starts as a stimulus that elicits an emotion/reaction that is then transformed into a feeling that becomes a thought. Thereafter, it is transformed into a symbol that is integrated into the psyche. Thus, trauma follows a path where an emotion, such as fear or rage, or a stimulus – such as a sound or an image that is related to the traumatic event – is dissociated in the complexes. This is mainly because the traumatic event is so chaotic and terrifying to our psyche that it has no choice but to dissociate.

Jungian Advanced Motor Processing© helps reintegrate what was once raw, unintegrated, emotionally triggering, and disturbing material brought on by the trauma. The integration process starts a deep change in the individual's psyche, a process of profound integration, what Jung would call "Individuation." Thus, the person will be able to be in their bodies and not dissociated from their bodies. Through the ability to be in one's own body and not dissociated, the person can finally experience inner harmony and begin to heal. This allows the trauma sufferer to move forward with their lives with a freedom that has not been experienced for a very long time.

What does JAMP© (AL-SAMARRAI, 2020) Treat?

This treatment has been studied and is known to be highly effective in reducing the following negative effects of dis-regulated emotional states and psychological disorders:

- Anger
- Sadness
- Numbness
- Confusion
- Worry
- Fear
- Hurt
- Negative Beliefs
- Disbelief
- Rage
- Anxiety
- Minimization
- Denial
- Pain
- Revulsion
- Guilt
- Shame
- Betrayal
- Withdrawal

- Jealousy
- Despair
- Self-Blame
- Doubt
- Revenge
- Brain Fog
- Physical Discomfort
- Dissociation
- Shame
- Trauma
- Complex Trauma
- PTSD
- Anxiety
- Body Image
- Stress
- Negative Thinking Patterns
- Negative Self Talk
- Self-Hate
- Panic Attacks

- Sexual Trauma
- Sexual Assault symptoms
- Physical Trauma
- Childhood Abuse
- Childhood Sexual Abuse
- Phobias
- Body Dysmorphic Disorder
- Eating Disorders
- Disturbing Thoughts & Memories
- Flashbacks
- Dissociative Disorders
- Psychosomatic Disorders
- Transitioning off of Psychotropic Medications
- Sleep Disturbances
- Self-Esteem
- Self-Defeating Behaviors
- Embarrassment
- Panic Disorders

Why JAMP© (AL-SAMARRAI, 2020)?

There is a great deal of psychic pain that affects the majority of people around the world. Many people reach a point in their lives where they feel the need to transform their lives and the lives of those around them.

Using JAMP© can help most people put their past – including all of their traumas, pain, perceived failures, and losses – to rest.

It will help you move forward with your whole self to a better life. It will transform you into the amazing, wonderful person you truly are.

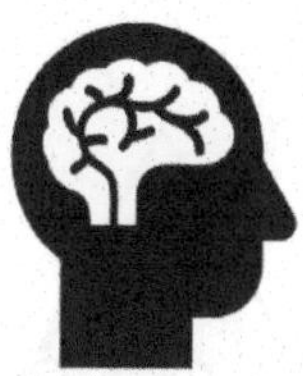

DR. LAHAB AL-SAMARRAI
CHRISTY FOSTER

JAMP©& The Resolution of the Glitch

CHAPTER 1 – THE ILLUSION

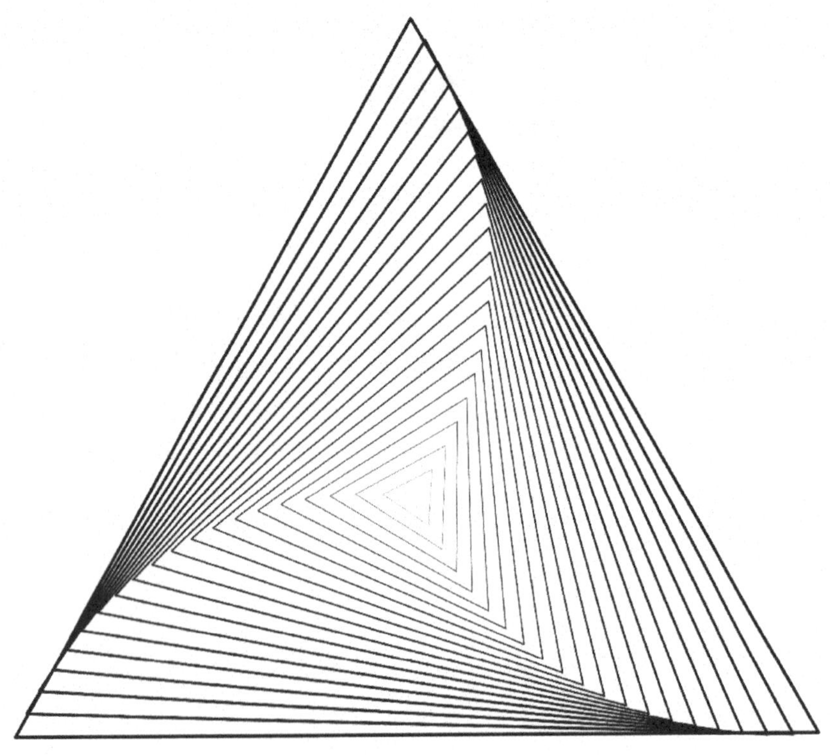

Chapter 1

The illusion of existence is one that has the ability to shroud your view of the world around you. You could live upwards of 70 years – you could even be one of the few centennials out there – and have all of these memories of what used to be. You cling to these memories and then, suddenly, it's all gone. Many of you may have read about or heard about this age-old trope that the elderly will usually lie on their deathbeds and flashback to a bygone era when they were younger and everything was copacetic. In simpler terms, the fondest memories that they have of their lives – or the most prominent and painful – are those that took place decades in their past. But what happened between the instant that those memories were formed and this precipice between the land of the living and the great beyond? Before we can get into that answer, let's look at a few more questions:

- What is the illusion of this life that we've been living?
- Why do we keep photographs of it as keepsakes?
- Why do we record videos in a bid to remember the "good times?"
- Why do we feel the need to talk about it and remember it?
- Does it really exist past the point of our physical exit from this world?

The real and honest truth of it all is that, whether you believe that this is all real and relevant – all of this that is going on in your life – it is all a part of your growth. However, if you spend the majority of your life stuck in a memory, you don't have the opportunity to make any more. The growth of the human soul occurs when we figure out who we are within this illusion. The illusion in itself is real because we are real. We have real relationships. None of it is real and all of it is real.

The quest should be to remember who we are without the weight of the stories and memories of our lives. We should be able to discard what people told us we should be or shouldn't be. We should be able to find the essence of who we are without the grip of the tribes that we grew up in.

All of those added elements in our lives – the career, the car, the familial upbringing, the trauma, the memories – are part of the illusion, not the essence. While all of those elements are a part of us, we are this being that is separate from it all. After all, when we leave this earth, all that is left is the illusion. It's like a fairytale or a myth that never really existed. That shouldn't frighten you. It should empower you to live a life on your terms that is defined by who you truly are.

So, let's explore this further. How is it possible to live on this earth for almost 100 years while shrouded in the illusion of memories?

Counting Down From 100

We, as human beings, are incredibly complex creatures when it comes to our minds. This is neither by design nor is it as nature intended, but a result of a series of events on a much larger scale throughout the history of time. We have come to value the past – seeking ourselves within it – or looking toward the future in a bid to motivate ourselves toward it. However, you don't need to motivate yourself toward the future. The future is coming, whether you like it or not. Tomorrow is around the corner, as is next month and next year. What we fail to understand is that living in the present as our most authentic selves is the only way to do away with the past and create a better future. Plots, plans, and schematics don't create better futures. Humans that are whole create better futures.

Now, here's another question for you: Would you allow something that happened 1,000 years ago to control your quality of life in this present moment? We're willing to bet that your answer to that is "no." It doesn't make any sense, does it? Who in their right mind would allow something that happened centuries ago to control their present and their future? It might seem nonsensical, but almost everyone does it. How so? Well, time is relative. The things that happened when you were 3 years old or 13 years old, or whenever else it was, might as well have been 1,000 years ago. Think about it logically for a minute. When you were a child, time seemed to drag on forever. The joys of summer felt like a lifetime but so did the 5 minutes until the school bell rang. Now that you're older, 5 minutes go by in a flash. Vacation time never feels long enough and it feels like you've blinked and an entire year has whizzed past you.

This notion that time heals all wounds is bogus. You heal your wounds. You remember who you were and unlearn your trauma patterns. What time does is that it puts a wedge between what happened and who you are right now because when we remember things, we're most likely not even remembering the moment that it happened. We're remembering the last time that we remembered it. And, so on it goes. The next time you remember something it will be a memory of the last remembering. So, essentially, as time goes on your view of this past experience – whether it's good or bad – becomes distorted. The act of remembering might not even trigger you as much anymore because you become so desensitized to the rumination. However, the trigger that lies within that past experience is still there –

unintegrated on the outside of who you are, yet controlling how you engage with yourself and the world around you. This means that whether something happened 1,000 years ago or 10 years ago, the only difference between the two is that you lived through one moment and not the other. Other than this, it should have very little significance on your ability to live a whole and healthy life. Except it does.

This brings us back to one of the first questions that we asked you. What happens between the moments that the elderly person on their deathbed remembers and the point of death? The answer to that is simple: they stop living. Something happens to them at the age of 40, for example, and they spend the next 30+ years repeating the same day over and over again. They remain stuck in a glitch of:

- Trauma;
- Lost love;
- Better times;
- Wondering why something happened;
- Reminiscing;
- Playing the story out with different endings;
- Trying to resolve a situation that no longer exists;
- And more.

Eventually, as we'll come to reveal in a later chapter, the glitch becomes comfortable. This repetition, or cycle, of reliving the trauma in different ways on different days, becomes familiar and there is comfort in the familiar. So, when you count back from year 100, you find that the vast majority of those years were spent while fully immersed in the illusion instead of being lived.

The goal should then be to remove ourselves from the glitch as early on as we can. That way, we can remember who we are.

Remembering Who You Are

Remembering who you are is a process of un-remembering or unlearning. We don't want to erase the trauma or pretend that it never occurred. Nor do we want to forget the good times and devalue them. Everything that has happened has played a role in your life. Every reaction that you have had has served a purpose. Every survival mechanism that you cultivated has guided you out of some tough situations. However, now that you are past that point, do you really want to live your life stuck in survival mode? We're willing to bet, just by the fact that you're here reading this book, that you want something more out of life. Discovering or remembering who you are in your purest form – beyond the shackles of the illusion – is where you will find your true north. This is where you will feel whole within yourself.

To return to this feeling of being whole, you need to be able to reconnect the unconscious and the conscious parts of yourself. You need to reintegrate shards of your personality that splintered off during past experiences and trauma. More often than not, when you feel conflicted it is because the unconscious and conscious pieces of yourself are not connected. This disconnect happens as we age because when we're born, we have no care in the world for ego-driven tasks. We don't care about what brand of diapers we're wearing or if we look a little silly. In fact, looking silly is expected and applauded in infancy. When an infant tries to crawl and wobbles back over onto their side, the adults in the room are in awe. When a child stands for the first time and falls on their backside, the adults are still in awe. When a child tries to walk and falls over more times than those in the room can count, they are still in awe. When we are born, the world hasn't had enough time to impose its will on us. We haven't had the time to allow our psyche to be manipulated and shifted away from our sense of self. We are all born with this original sense of wholeness and unity. We're on "factory settings" if you will. However, the factory isn't pumping out carbon copies. It's sending completely unique individuals into the world who are whole and centered within themselves. What happens, thereafter, is that the world and, most often, our tribe get their hands on us. Then, all of a sudden, no one claps for us anymore. We're told to sit up straight. We're told not to eat, walk, talk, move, or breathe in a certain way. We're taught how to be presentable and how to perform for the outside world and, so, the ego is born.

This is one of the many reasons why you might find yourself living in a world of ideation and rumination. You, like so many other people, were born onto a stage. This stage applauded you for the basic and beautiful feats of learning to walk but put you in line with what everyone else is meant to do as soon as you could speak. You learned, from very early on, that it matters more what other people think of you and whether they perceive you as someone well-mannered who plays by the rules. While societal rules aren't inherently bad, it's how and what you were taught that made you move away from your sense of self – allowing your ego to take center stage. What this means is that trauma can be twofold. It can involve a single act that frightens us and confuses us. This trauma then repeats itself as a memory. Then there is the trauma of the loss of self, which usually stems from what we've been taught about ourselves in relation to the world around us.

You might be thinking, "Well, how do I remember myself in my purest form if I can't remember what that purity of infancy was like?" That's a fair question. Another might be, "Do I really know who my true self is?" The good news is that although it might be too far back to remember in the sense of the word, we can unpack this true nature of our souls by collapsing the complexes that stop our true archetypes from coming forward. For this, we need to look at the architecture of the soul.

The Architecture of The Soul

Jungian Advanced Motor Processing, or JAMP© (AL-SAMARRAI, 2020) for short, is based on the works of the founding father of analytical psychology, Carl Gustav Jung. When it comes to remembering who we once were in our purest forms, we need to understand his principles of "The Archetypes." These archetypes are inborn personalities and behavioral traits that form a connection to our true self and should not be confused with the 12 Archetypes such as the great mother and the hero. We won't get into those at this point because we want to explore how you can resolve the glitch by returning to your truest self. With that in mind, the archetypes that we are interested in are:

- The Persona;
- The Shadow/The Unknown Other;
- The Anima/Animus;
- The Ego;
- The Self.

The persona is how you present yourself to the world. It is the face that you put on – one that you believe is widely accepted and serves everyone's best interests, especially your own. When the persona and the true self are too dissimilar, it becomes all too easy to lose sight of the true self altogether. What happens then is that you have these complexes – traumas and tribal influencing – that are neither a part of the persona or the self. **However, the traumas hang above the archetypes encapsulated by the complex as a protective shield and hangs like a satellite in orbit, sapping up all** of the energy of the archetype. In order to return to the Self, we need to study the architecture and dynamics of the complex so that we can collapse it on itself. Only then will that energy – which can neither be created nor destroyed – is return to the archetype and breathe life back into it.

So, here we answer the question: "How do we return to our true selves when we can't remember them?" When you remove the satellites which are the complexes, or traumas, that automatically triggers a re-energizing of the attack on the Self. As we become whole within the Self, the ego, the trauma, and the complexes themselves are absorbed back into the Archetype of the Self. However, the Complexes will shrink down in form but will leave a distant echo that we are able to function as whole individuals that are driven by the Archetype of the Self, without any interference from the "satellite" that is the complex.

The Unknown Other, on the other hand, is the chaotic and murkier side of our psyche that we often live in denial of. You see, we cannot fathom the idea of being the wrongdoer/bad/scary/ugly and often bury these sides of ourselves in The Unknown Other. This suppression inflates this Unknown Other and it often gets projected onto other people. This is why we refer to it as "the unknown other" not the Shadow. In the pursuit of becoming one's true self, embracing all aspects of our psyche – and all archetypes – is the only way to allow the self to flourish, but we'll discuss this in more detail later on.

Next, come the anima and the animus. The animus is the masculine aspect in women while the anima is the feminine aspect in men. For many of us, we were told that boys don't play with dolls or wear pink. Good girls don't get their Sunday dresses muddy and tattered. That's just how things were way back when. However, this turns into self-inflicted trauma. The human psyche knows nothing about gender roles at birth. It wants to explore the feminine within the masculine and vice versa.

Finally, there is the self which encompasses everything from the ego to the unconscious and the conscious elements of the psyche. Therefore, to be whole – to be whole within the self – the archetypes need to be allowed their space within the self. The complexes around the archetypes – what we refuse to accept in our Unknown Other, what we believe someone of our gender should and shouldn't do, and the persona we believe is worthy of being out in the world – needs to be reabsorbed into the self.

The journey away from the glitch starts with the journey toward pulling the shards back into place so that the whole entire self can be mended at the fracture sites.

*

As we progress, we are going to go deeper into the psyche. Just as we began with the illusion and ended up at the Self, this journey will take you through the unraveling of ties that bind you to the illusion that has you believing that your persona is your true self. You will rediscover your true north by reabsorbing the energy that has been taken away from the self and given to the traumas that keep you in the glitch and place far too much emphasis on the archetypes as separate forms. They should, in fact, be a part of the whole self and this is where we begin laying the groundwork for JAMP© (AL-SAMARRAI, 2020).

CHAPTER 2 – THE BEGINNING, THE END, AND THE STORY IN BETWEEN

Chapter 2

As we move away from the illusion of reality as we see it, we also need to be able to address time. This is something that we touched on briefly in the previous chapter, but it's imperative that we delve a little deeper. Time is something completely non-linear that we view in a very linear fashion because we believe that we can quantify it. To be fair, it can be quantified in the sense that we can see our days transition from morning into evening and we can see the seasons shift. What we're really talking about here, however, is the time we have within our own lifespans. Now, we say that it's non-linear because if it were truly linear, we would be able to move from one point to the next with our pasts planted firmly behind us. Yet, here we are, discussing the very issue of constantly circling back to past trauma, belief systems, and ideologies.

The conundrum that we're then faced with is the cessation of self within the time that we have within our lifespans. This is where many glitches can be found. As time passes and we age, there will be many instances when the people that we have come to be cease to exist. This is something that we refer to as "little deaths" and these little deaths occur in everyone's lives. But what exactly is a little death and how does it impact us?

To answer this question, we must come back to the understanding of time within our lifespans. We are under the illusion that we are born once and that we die once and that everything in between is part of this one life that we've been given. What we fail to recognize or acknowledge are the dozens of little deaths that we experience throughout our lives. We're not referring to the deaths of those we love who move on from the physical plane of reality before us. We're referring to our own deaths – yes, plural. So, let's explore this before we get into the depths of defining reality.

When you're born, you come into this world as a newborn who can see without knowing. You pick up on audible cues and, eventually, visual cues that come in the form of facial expressions. Thereafter, the newborn dies and gives way to the infant. When the infant dies, the toddler is born. When the toddler dies, the child is born. When the child dies, the teen is born and so on it goes right up until you reach adulthood. When we reach a certain age that is deemed an adult age, we suddenly think that we are done growing. We feel that we are done evolving and that we can settle into this persona for the rest of our days on this earth. The problem with this theory is that age doesn't actually define which phase of our lives we've entered. It is entirely dependent on experience. Yes, there are milestones that an infant should reach by their first birthday to be seen as "developmentally on track" to move onto the toddler phase of their lives, but we falsely believe that this has to do with the passage of time. In fact, it has more to do with the individual infant and their experiences in the lead-up to that first-year milestone.

If we look at it this way, we can see that while we can see a definite beginning, middle, and end to physical life, we don't actually see the actual birth and death that someone experiences throughout their lives. Just think about a child. Whether you're a parent yourself or an aunt or uncle or even if you have friends with kids. As a parent, you can look back on videos of your child in their younger years and it will feel like you're looking at a completely different person. If you have friends with children, you could go away for years and come back to find someone who hasn't just physically changed but mentally and spiritually as well. On the other end of that spectrum, when someone we love dies, they don't merely cease to exist. Yes, their bodies are no longer with us in the physical realm. We can't reach out and touch them. We can't see them whenever we'd like. We can't pick up the phone and call them. However, that doesn't mean that the connection that you had with them ceases. If anything, it moves to a different level as their transition out of the physical realm also transforms you and you might experience a little death as you lose the physical version of them.

In that light, we need to define reality and what is real to us because this is all subjective to each individual out there. Let's move on and discuss this.

Defining Reality

A little earlier we spoke of the expectation to reach certain milestones by a certain age in the early phases of our lives and how this developmental expectation ceases when we reach what we deem as adulthood. This is why the more advanced we become as a civilization, the more we regress into this entrapment within our own glitches. The glitches show up more often and hold us back because we have these preconceived notions of what should happen in our lives and when. We overgeneralize and feel "less than" or inadequate in some way if we don't reach these made-up milestones. Of course, these milestones were created with the best of intentions as we sought to understand our own developmental processes from birth and beyond. However, in seeking this knowledge, we boxed ourselves into these timelines that create expectations according to the passage of time and not according to experiences. As such, we think that once we reach adulthood, these little deaths stop occurring, but there are just as many moments in our adult lives when we shed the skin of our old selves and move into a completely new persona.

When we hold on to who we were or what happened in the past, we carry a reanimated corpse around with us. As you continue to age and you unwittingly experience these little deaths, you continue to carry more and more reanimated corpses around with you. The result is a heaviness that almost gravitationally pulls you back to your glitches without you even realizing it. Ultimately, you remain trapped in an illusion of reality that is based on past selves that are just begging to be laid to rest. Just as we mentioned with regard to losing a loved one, to lay your past self to rest doesn't mean that your connection to that past self no longer exists. This newer version of yourself was built on the backbone of all your past selves and experiences. Nonetheless, it can be difficult to transition between the death of your past self and the birth of your new self. It can actually become a traumatic event if not handled with care. With that in mind, let's detail a few common little deaths while keeping in mind not to overgeneralize:

- The end of a career.
- Stepping away from a religion.
- The end of a relationship.
- The loss of a loved one.
- Moving cities.
- Injury and the loss of mobility.
- The loss of a talent or gift.
- Selling a home.

It's important to note that these are a handful of examples in a virtually endless list of possible deaths that one could experience in their life. This in itself is one of the main pillars in the understanding that reality is completely subjective. One might even argue that there is no such thing as reality. Even in a conversation between two people that have common interests, their experience of that conversation is going to be completely different.

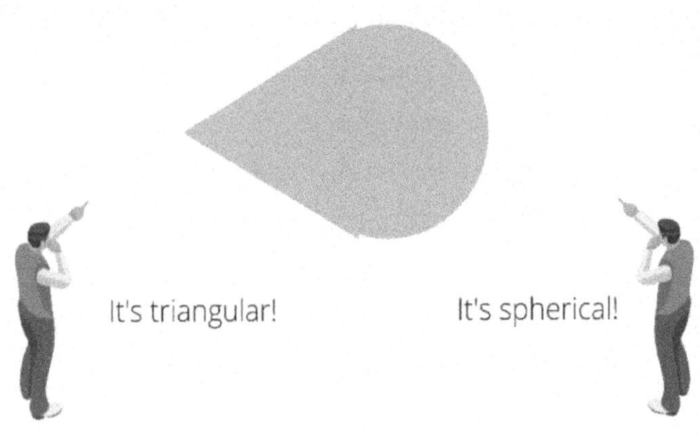

Therefore, we cannot expect to experience the same little deaths as the person beside us. We cannot even expect to transition through death and rebirth in the same way as the person beside us just because they've experienced something similar. For instance, you and your best friend could experience the loss of a parent around the same time, but you will not go through the same transitionary stages as them. There are many factors in play that will determine the reality of their transition by comparison to your own. One would need to consider how close they were to that parent, how they process loss, how the conditioning of their upbringing determines their way of mourning, and much more.

This begs the question: what is reality?

We tend to take the very literal meaning of the word by assuming that reality is what is "real." We believe that the only things around us that are real are things that we can physically touch or quantify and because we falsely believe that we can quantify time, we think that time is real. This ties in with those milestones that we looked at earlier. However, reality is relative to each person and when there is a fallout between what we expect to be real and who we are, there is another glitch. How does this link to the restoration of self and the removal of the satellites around our archetypal structures? Well, when we accept that nothing is "real" and, yet, all of it is, we are able to release the glitch. When we know that how we perceive ourselves, how we view ourselves as being perceived by others, and how they actually perceive us are all incongruent, we free ourselves of timelines, milestones, and expectations. We move into a space where we are able to embrace the twin or polar spectrums of the birth-death archetype and are able to live presently. That is the goal, after all, to move back within. To remember who we were before the conditioning and before the expectations of what others tell us is real. It is the reabsorption of who we are into the self.

Accepting that these external factors are none of our business and that our only business revolves around this return to self will help us move on from the little death without invalidating it. This brings us to reality stasis.

Living in Reality Stasis

Let's quickly recap before we unpack the undertones of reality stasis. First, we experience many little deaths throughout our lives. Second, our perception of reality needs to come from within and not from what we suspect the world expects of us or perceives us as. That is how we are able to do away with reality stasis.

What is reality stasis?

Reality stasis occurs when our identity-tie to the past is much stronger than our identity-tie to the present. It can also occur when our identity-tie to the future is much stronger than our tie to the present, but it most often occurs when we are bound by our past. It can be incredibly strong and overbearing where we are aware of this bind. However, it can also be quite subtle, where we don't necessarily realize that this tie is present. For instance, you could find yourself in a position where you are struggling to let go of a past relationship. The relationship might have been, from your perspective, incredibly happy and fulfilling or incredibly toxic. Whatever the case may be, you find yourself struggling to let go of this relationship.

In the case where you found that the relationship was happy and fulfilling, you might be in a mental predicament where you think you will never find that happiness with anyone ever again. You might think that you have lost your one true love and that there is no possible way to let go of them. You might even find yourself wishfully waiting for the opportune moment to win them back. By holding onto this past relationship, you are preventing yourself from mourning the end of the relationship. You can go years with this idea of this romance in your heart that simply no longer exists. Yes, your connection to the experiences you shared with that person is very valid. However, you are no longer physically attached to them. While there is no time limit on love, there needs to be a moment of transition where you allow the experience to show you something about yourself that you weren't previously aware of. When this happens, you can release the past relationship, accept it for what it was, and transition to the next phase of your life. It's not about forgetting the person you were or the person you were with. It's not about invalidating the love that was once shared. It's about allowing this new version of yourself to emerge. Leaving your past self in the past with that past love allows the new you to find new love. Now, this is a very interesting topic because people can manipulate themselves into thinking that by letting go of someone, they are being unfaithful to that person or themselves. This is mainly due to the fairytale trope that we feed ourselves. There isn't one true love for you anymore than there is one true "you" throughout your life. More importantly, what you often miss in a past relationship is the version of yourself that you were with that particular person. It's not even about the person you were with! In some cases, it is the fear that if we allow the past to lay where it is that we are killing off a piece of ourselves. It is the inherent fear of death that keeps us frozen and clinging to the past because by being present and moving forward we get closer to the "big death."

Other than holding onto a relationship that you perceived as happy and fulfilling, there is the issue of holding onto a relationship that was, perhaps, toxic. You can see this in the form of projecting your fear of being hurt in the same way onto the person that is attempting to come into your life in the present moment. This form of reality stasis will keep you trapped in the memory of the trauma of the relationship. It will keep you from falling into the same trappings of a similar relationship but it will also prevent you from moving on to the next phase of your life. Instead of choosing not to enter into a new relationship because you are not interested in being with anyone, in particular, you'll avoid a new relationship based on past trauma. And this doesn't just apply to relationships, but to almost every single facet of life.

When we hold onto the past, we essentially prevent the evolution of our souls from taking place. Whether your purpose is to help others, create change in your community, or simply just to exist at peace, the little deaths that occur are necessary for you to achieve your purpose. To hang onto something that has only been brought into our sphere of "reality" to help us move forward is completely counterintuitive and is how we remain trapped in a circle instead of moving through the spiral. It doesn't matter how far forward you have walked away from your past because as soon as you begin to look back with longing, sadness, anger, or resentment, you're already right back where you started. The past will suck you back in time and time again unless you make the conscious effort to keep that forward momentum. You have to make the choice to carry on even when the reason is unclear as to why something has happened the way that it did.

*

Ultimately, there is a beginning and end and everything in between. However, it is not the beginning of physical life and the big death. There is the beginning of a new version of yourself as the result of the death of the old version. That particular death will almost always come in the form of the end of an era in your life that is followed by a period of mourning before a rebirth. The goal should always be to live as presently as possible without getting sucked back in by the winds of the past. This is the only way you can move past the glitch and your identity-tie to the past which keeps you in a recurring loop.

CHAPTER 3 – THE INVISIBLE PRISON

The invisible prison is one of the areas that need to be addressed with JAMP© (AL-SAMARRAI, 2020) in order to release yourself from the glitch. This prison that keeps us caged in our own minds comes in the form of trying to make sense of the past. It can feel incredibly tempting to try and assess or analyze what was instead of focusing on the present and we tell ourselves that we are doing this to heal ourselves. As we progress, we will discuss the idea of things happening "to" you and how this mentality reinforces your invisible prison, but first, we must discuss the human signature.

As human beings, we all have an energetic signature. This is a unique set of frequencies that are within each of us. These frequencies are sometimes referred to as the soul or the essence of who we are. They determine our interactions with the world and our ability to process information. The problem comes in when we experience deep trauma that impacts our frequency on multiple levels and forces this energy signature back within us. Instead of emitting our energetic signature, it becomes caged in a heavy and invisible prison.

We need to look at it this way. When you experience trauma, you are bound to absorb some of the energy of the object or person that inflicted the trauma upon you. If you were in a car wreck, you might absorb some of the energy of the initial impact and keep it in your body long after your physical wounds have healed. If you were emotionally or verbally abused as a child, you might keep the trauma in your body long after you've done the work to do away with the negative beliefs that were imprinted on you via the verbal onslaught. This can begin to manifest itself as physical pain and illness that reduces the size of your cage and leaves you feeling like you can barely move, let alone breathe within your own skin. As such, you need to be able to remove this energy that was imposed upon you before you can unblock your own energy. Your body will keep the memory of the trauma as the primary conduit for your energetic energy in this plain of reality. What this means is that you will have difficulty with releasing that trauma and moving away from the glitch because not only are you mentally reliving the trauma, but physically and energetically as well.

The invisible prison is, therefore, threefold: mental, energetic, and physical in nature. In an effort to unlock the prison door, you have to start focusing more on your role in the trauma and not the role of the inflictor. I'm sure you're wondering what role you could have possibly played in being traumatized and before we're accused of victim-blaming, allow us to explain.

Why Is This Happening to Me

In the previous chapter, we looked at the little deaths and how it's necessary to let go of past relationships, whether they were fulfilling during their lifecycle or toxic. This would be a great example to begin with as it is the most obvious of them all and the easiest to absorb. If you were in a relationship – platonic or romantic – that came to an end, are you viewing the lifecycle of the relationship through your own eyes or those of the other party? While there are many layers to how this is linked to your energetic signature, the first layer involves looking at how you participated in the relationship. If this relationship and its final demise are two of the glitches that you remain stuck in, you need to cleanse yourself of the other party's energy before you can address your own energy and focus on the role that you played in the relationship. That seems fairly simple, but the second layer is looking at whether or not you were toxic in the relationship – if toxicity was the cause for the final demise or little death. This is where it gets a bit tricky to dive into where abuse is concerned because, of course, there is no time when the abused or the victims should have to say "what did I do wrong?" Nonetheless, you want to be in a position where you are in full ownership of your own energy and your position or role in the memory that keeps recurring. We'll tell you why.

The glitch wants you to keep reliving the past because that's how it stays alive within you. That is how it keeps your energetic signature in an invisible prison. So, when you recall the trauma or past event that you have not moved on from, the key that keeps the lock – well – locked is that you often try to make sense of what happened. Instead of remembering the trauma from how you truly felt or what you thought, there is the residual feeling of fear, anger, sadness, anxiety, or any other emotion that ran through you at the time, but the focus is always on "why did this happen to me?" "Why did they do this to me?" "What have I done to deserve this?" The energy and the power are always in the hands of the inflictor. We try to make sense of what happened, not by looking back on how it impacted us at the time and stepping back into our own shoes, but by becoming a voyeur that is looking for clues and answers. It's almost as if we're searching for hints as to what led to the situation in a bid to avoid it in the future. However, all that we do in the process of assessing for avoidance is that we end up reliving the trauma, but this time, at our own hands.

This is the prison: living in the memory of what happened to you and not how you participated in that moment. Trying to remedy your present by remedying your past is always going to be a tough one to navigate because there is a very fine line between healing your past and obsessing over it. The reason why it's important to heal your energy and purge the inflictor's energy is that your mind and body are connected and, more importantly, they don't know the difference between a memory and an actual event. Yes, you know for a fact that the person that was physically abusive toward you isn't standing in the room with you and abusing you right now, but when you relive it, you put yourself through the same physiological and mental responses that you experienced the first time around.

To let go of the trauma glitch, you need to revisit it just one more time. Close your eyes and actually recall the event. When you think of this situation or retrace this memory, do you cringe? Do grimace? Do you flinch? Where do you feel the heaviest in your body? These are the areas where the inflictor imprinted their energy upon you and these are the areas that you need to reprogram when the memory comes up. You need to release the tension in your body in these areas as the memory comes up. Unfurrow your brow, breathe deeply into the areas that are tense, and release this energy that doesn't belong to you. If you feel anxious, repeat the word "calm" in your mind or out loud as you do this. If you feel afraid, repeat the word "safe" as you do this. Remove the energy and fill the wounded area with your own positive energy. Only then will you be able to revisit the memory without reexperiencing the trauma. It will be somewhat like watching a movie. You can view it without being energetically invested in it. When the movie ends, you can leave the mental cinema without feeling drained, congested, heavy, or charged. This will also allow you to recall the event without the distortion of the glitch.

The Trauma Glitch

Have you ever tried to watch a scary movie through your fingers in a bid to hide from the scenes or character depictions that seem a little too scary for your liking? If you have, then you'll know the all-too-familiar view through the little bars that are your fingers. Trauma works in the same way. When we recall our trauma without positioning ourselves in the role that we held at the time and only view it from above, we view it through our fingers. We raise our hands to shield ourselves from seeing the act in full view. When you can't see the trauma clearly, it becomes distorted. You don't remember the event for what it actually was because:

1. It is too frightening to remember and to play the tape all the way to the end.
2. Your eyes were shut half the time as you flinched.

What our psyche does is that it tries to fill in the gaps in order to make sense of it all, but our minds can be quite deceptive. This isn't an intentional or malicious act but rather a side-effect of how imaginative our minds truly are. We embellish. Due to the fact that the trauma was so unexpected and such a violation of our true selves, we cannot understand it. When you're able to unlock the invisible prison – to remove your hands from your eyes so that they are neither blinders nor cage bars – you can understand the trauma and see it as it was.

If this does not happen, you are bound to experience psychosomatic issues of a very troubling kind. The more you revisit your trauma with shielded eyes, the more your body is going to attack the inflictor's energy within you. However, the energy, while very real in a vibrational sense, is not real in a physical sense. So, what ends up happing is that your body attacks itself in the regions where the inflictor's energy is present. The only way to stop this from happening is to remove that energy altogether by breathing into the wound and evacuating the energy which does not belong to you. The psychosomatic issues you could be facing as a result of not dealing with this include autoinflammatory and autoimmune conditions, aches, pains, chronic illnesses of the nervous system as well as the gut, and much more.

When it comes to actually healing illnesses of a psychosomatic kind, you need to be able to walk through the fire first before it can be purged through your system. Looking back, at this juncture, is important but you have to be doing it in a way that allows you to process and digest the illness – whether physical or mental – that was caused by the trauma. If you're looking back to reminisce or because your body and psyche are addicted to the trauma and the drama you remain locked in the circular prison.

The fire in this case represents the conscious desire to change the narrative that plays in your mind repeatedly. The fire represents the treatment or steps that you will take to remove yourself from the prison. It comes from the willingness to go through the initial transformative discomfort and burning of the change as you relinquish these energies and these old versions of yourself. The burning always comes first. The little death always comes first. You have to be willing to jump in headfirst before you come out the other side as a transformed individual. As you'll come to see as we progress with the steps in this book, the only way to true healing is to address all facets of the individual – of yourself. You are a whole person. Your being is a delicate ecosystem. When one area is out of balance, it sends a ripple effect throughout your entire being. To address emotional abuse, you need to address the emotional and psychosomatic effects that have arisen as a result of that initial abuse. The problem that most people have is that they seek to treat one facet of the being. When you're in a car wreck, the focus is on treating your physical wounds with just a hint of trauma counseling. The treatment for the fracture to your spiritual self and the removal of the energy that was imparted on you is lost.

Where trauma and the glitch are concerned, there is no removal of the glitch without addressing each of the facets of your being that were impacted by the trauma. In essence, you're giving your energetic frequency – in all senses of the term – a once over without shifting your focus away from the self and toward the trauma. The focus should always be on you and not just on recalling the event that happened "to you."

*

Once you've unlocked the invisible prison, you'll have the clear vision that is necessary to see your trauma for what it was. In so doing, there is no longer a missing piece of the puzzle that your psyche feels the need to resolve. It is the first tangible step in unraveling the trauma glitch. This will help you to change the glitch from a circle that keeps you stuck in a loop to a spiral that you can climb without getting sucked too far back into the trauma when you look back. This is where we kick off our next chapter as we enter The Spiral.

CHAPTER 4 – THE SPIRAL

Chapter 4

To enter the spiral, one has to be willing to move through their past traumas without allowing the glitch to interfere with that movement. It has to be as fluid as possible. You see, we all think that we are moving in a straight line from Point A to Point B – in other words, from birth to death. However, we are not in this linear experience. Just imagine that earth is as big as your living room. That's all that there is on this plane of reality. There is nothing beyond those four walls but the vastness of the universe and the countless galaxies within it. Now, you're in this living room after you are born at the front door. That is how you enter the world or, in this case, your living room. When you walk in, you find a bunch of people walking around in a perfect circle within hula hoops that are lying on the ground. Each person has a hoop. Some are a little bent and there are a variety of colors – well, some people have the same color. You see these people walking around in these circles and every time they've made a full revolution, they cry out in pain. They stop momentarily, cry it out, and then continue walking in circles. You some that are a little older getting closer to the opposite end of the room and every so often one of them will climb out the window – leaving their hoop behind – and then they'll climb down the fire escape into the great beyond. In your first couple of hours in that room, your parents are standing just ahead of you. They show you how to place your hoop down on the floor and inform you that in a couple of days, they'll be heading out the window and your job is to keep circling your hoop until you make it to the window as well. You question them. You question why those people keep crying out in pain and, sooner or later, one of your parents snaps and you recoil in emotional pain. Something strange happens at that moment. You look down at your hoop and there is a glowing light coming from it. There is an image of your face, as it looked in that moment, etched into the hoop. Half a day passes and you decide to talk to someone else in the room. Both of you forget about your hoops momentarily as you walk in circles alongside one another until one of you hurts the other and creates another etching in the other's hoop. Sure enough, a day goes past and one of your parents makes a sudden exit through the window on the other side of the room. Soon after your other parent follows. You're in the middle of the room and you begin to see why those other people were crying out in pain every time they made a revolution around their own hoops. They have been trapped in a circle of reliving past pain – pain that was etched into the hoop on the floor. It stood there as a reminder of the pain and they were unable to leave that hoop for most – if not all – of their lives.

At this point, you're wondering what all of this means. You're questioning the meaning of existence and you know that you cannot go, but you also don't feel ready to head out that window. You just want to exist in this precious moment without having to move through the circle, or cycle, that this hoop is keeping you trapped in. Suddenly, out of the corner of your eye, you see someone climbing a spiral staircase. The images that are etched into their hoop stream up into the air around their staircase but the glow of the imagery changes every time they come back around to it on their way up the spiral. You watch them for a few hours and realize that they are looking down at their hoop less and less. There is a trapdoor in the ceiling and a beautiful, bright sunny day beyond the door. They make their way up and, as you crane your neck to peer through the trapdoor, you see that there are still more stairs beyond the room. It's a continuous spiral and this person is ascending out of the room. The trapdoor shuts behind them and no one else in the room seems to have noticed their escape.

You pause and wonder how you might enter a spiral staircase of your own. The existence beyond the window seems so dark and uninviting. You want to ascend into that bright sunny day. Now, let's elaborate on what all of this means.

The room represents the earth. The front door is your birth and the window is your death. Technically, you move in a straight line toward the window as time passes. However, within your own existence, you keep circling back to your past. You cling to what your parents or other family members have told you during your formative hours (years) in that room and you relive painful experiences every time something happens that makes you look down at your hoop. By the time you reach that window, that hoop is going to be covered in imagery. You might move alongside someone for a while, you might even bump into someone's circle from time to time, and that all adds to your images or makes you recall past pain. This recollection, however, isn't always going to be in the form of revisiting the trauma like a movie that plays in your head. The images will be triggered into streaming when something similar occurs, but you will feel it in your body and in your emotions. While you move toward that window, you begin to develop a fear of what lies beyond it. It seems dark and cold. You might catch a glimpse of what life could be like if you changed your hoop into that spiral staircase, but what you might fail to realize – even right now – is that the sunny day above the room and the dark night beyond the window are all the same. Neither is better than the other and neither is scarier than the other. What matters is our perception in this life. Nothing has changed beyond the room for you or the person who is on the spiral staircase. The only difference between the two of you is how you perceive life and death. That is why the person on the spiral staircase is able to move beyond the cycle of their lives and view death as a natural step into the next realm of energetic existence while you feel as though you are trapped in fear with nothing but darkness awaiting you at the end of it all.

You might be thinking that if we are all going to the same place after we depart the physical world, what difference does it make whether we live a fulfilled life or not? There is a difference. It does matter. It matters to you. It matters to the people who walk through that door after you. It matters in terms of the energetic footprint that you leave behind when you're gone. It matters to you right now or you wouldn't even be reading this book! So, the goal should be to transcend the circle or cycle that is represented by the hula hoop and move on to the spiral staircase where you can experience life at different levels as time passes. Doing this will set you free from your past pain, stop the glitches from happening as well as the cries of pain, and give you the chance to step into who you truly are instead of just living the life you've been taught is meant for you.

What you have to realize is that enlightenment – life and everything it has to offer – is a non-linear experience.

Enlightenment is Non-Linear

The question on the tip of your tongue right now is, most likely, "How do I enter the spiral?" The simple answer would be "heal!" Healing, as we know, is not that simple. It can be if you use the tools that we will be providing you with, but you have to be so unwaveringly committed to your own growth that nothing stands in your way. That is the only way you can truly set yourself free from being so affected by everything that triggers the memory of your past pain and experiences.

Let's walk through a prime example of the glitch in action.

Past Trauma – Scenario 1

When you were about eight years old, you were out in the front yard, playing with your action figures. It was a normal day like any other, but from inside the house, you heard your parents fighting. It was unlike them to argue, and you stood up to see what all the fuss was about. This would be the first time that you experienced the snap in the room that is your world – just like in the scenario we looked at earlier in the chapter. You ran into the house, not knowing what was wrong, and found your mother crying in the kitchen while your father continued to yell at her. She yelled right back and you can barely remember what they were saying now that you're older. All you remember is your father turning around, and yelling at you to get out of the kitchen. He had never spoken to you this way before. It was like something had snapped inside of him. But you would soon become familiar with this tone of voice and the body language he was exhibiting. Now, for some odd reason, unbeknownst to you, you can't stand summer afternoons just before the fall. You seem to be tense and on edge around the house whenever you feel that cool, crisp air coupled with the dying warmth of summer. You find yourself unable to enjoy certain days and you often hear yourself saying to your spouse, "I don't know what's wrong with me. Something just feels off."

Welcome to the glitch.

The truth is, for many people, the glitches that they experience aren't overt in nature. They are silent just like this one. Why? Well, because you normalized the experience of witnessing your parents at each other's throats. You learned to just get on with life and continue playing with your action figures while they had screaming matches for all the neighborhood to hear. You might have been ostracized by the neighbors who didn't want their kids coming around to your house because you were "that" family. That one moment that was the beginning of your end of "normalcy" sets you off. It triggers you and you enter the emotional glitch. Your body tenses up just as it did that afternoon and you are unable to function as the so-called normal adult that you think you've evolved into.

Past Trauma – Scenario 2

Your trauma becomes more overtly visible as you have children of your own. You find yourself in a situation where you either shut down completely or tell them – in a harsh tone – to leave the room whenever you and their other parent are having a conversation that you believe is not age appropriate for them. You're trying to shield them from witnessing what you did as a child, but you're scaring them in the process and repeating the cycle, despite your best efforts.

Sometimes it's a time of year, a word, a song, or a similar situation that triggers the reaction and sends you back into the glitch. Whatever it may be, it is also the best place to find insight into what is pulling you back. It's easy to be cool, calm, and collected when life is going our way. However, if we have the willpower to dive deeper when we are triggered, that is how we will come to understand what makes us tick. That is when you can take it all apart to put it back together again. That is how you break the hula hoop so that you can elevate a part of it and create the first step on your spiral staircase.

Entering the spiral is something that can promote your healing, but you have to find a way to activate it and enter it first. It promotes your healing because it allows you to move away from the images that are etched into that hula hoop on the floor. The further away you get from those glitches, the more enlightened and literally lighter you will feel. For this part, you will need to stand in your truth.

Standing in Truth

I want you to think of the glitch as a big bully. The more you recoil and turn away from it, the more power it has over you. This bully, however, cannot climb stairs. It's afraid of the heights of enlightenment. The only place it belongs is right where it is and will not be able to follow you past the first few steps on your staircase. This is why many people experience the glitch once they've begun their healing and mistakenly think that they are not progressing. You will come back to your triggers but the severity of your reaction to them will begin to dwindle the higher up the spiral you go. You will have to stand and face your glitch. You will need to look it in the eye and size it up. It is going to flex on you. It is going to threaten to beat you up and stuff you in your locker, but it can't. It's all talk and no action. At that moment of being triggered, you only need to override your fear for 60 seconds. That's all it takes for it to stop tricking you into thinking that it can hurt you. Then you give it a good once over and learn what about it actually scares you or triggers you. When you have the answer to that, you'll most likely see that there is nothing in your present life that the glitch has the power to take away. It cannot take away your voice. It cannot physically hurt you. It cannot end your life as you know it. It can't make you hide away in your bedroom and cover your head with a pillow until it goes away. Realizing this will help you take the first step. To do this without the pain of desensitization treatment, you need treatment. Until then, the glitch will repeat itself until you find a way to face it and learn from it. Sometimes, simply asking yourself a question will help you stand in your truth at that moment. When you feel a swelling of anxiety due to a trigger, stop and ask:

- What am I feeling right now?
- What do I have to be scared of right now?
- Is there a real threat present?
- What does this feeling remind me of?
- When was the last time I felt like this?
- When was the first time I felt like this?

These questions help bring to light what caused the glitch in the first place and having that "aha" moment will give you the strength to say, "This isn't my truth anymore."

*

Standing in your truth is only the beginning of your journey. Detaching your identity from the glitch is the next step. This is one of the hardest things that you will have to do because we tend to think that our identity is centered around our glitches. We say that our glitches made us who we are today and that is simply not true. Experiences don't shape our personalities or alter our archetypes. Our personalities or archetypes are responsible for how we handle and overcome those glitches. They are not a part of us and you can remove them. We'll see why this is important up next.

CHAPTER 5 – DETACHING YOUR IDENTITY FROM THE GLITCH

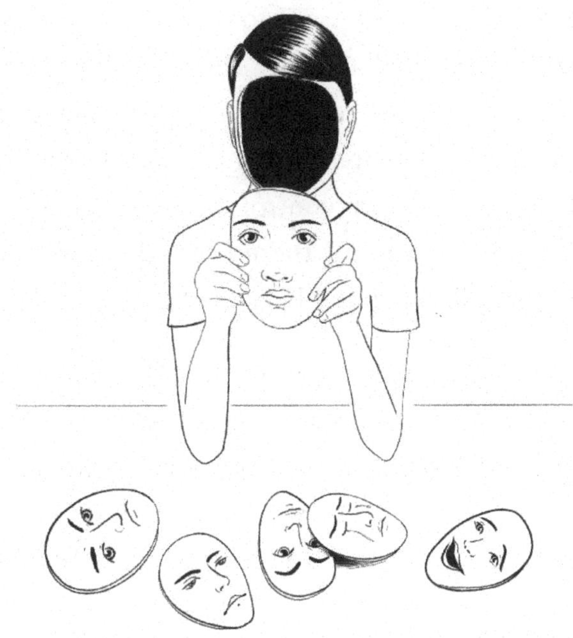

Looking back at your past is one of the glitch's key ways of keeping you trapped in a cycle. When we cling to the past, we lose sight of the present moment, and, before we know it, we're knee-deep in the future. The problem with this passage of time – while walking around with proverbial blinders on – is that you are no longer in control of your life. Let's discuss this for a minute. According to Carl Jung, and many other notable psychologists as well as philosophers, there is an imbalance between two ideologies. The first is that we are completely in control of our own lives. The second is the idea that we need to wait for permission from some force unknown to us to start living our lives at the helm. That is a conundrum in and of itself: we are in control, but we are not. We want to pave the way for our futures, yet we're stuck in autopilot mode. The fact is we can change our lives for the better. We can return to our truest selves and embrace the. While there are archetypes that we all fall into, that doesn't mean that we are not in control of what we do with these personalities. Furthermore, if there is anything in control of our destinies, it certainly shouldn't be a glitch.

There is another scenario we would like you to linger on. Let's say your mother was a drug addict while she was pregnant with you. You come into this world and you are already addicted to the hard drugs that she had taken while you were in utero. As a baby, you have no way of overcoming this other than with the care and comfort of someone to hold you through this horrible withdrawal that you are experiencing – something that someone else inflicted on you. This person, who was meant to love and protect you, has harmed you before you've even taken your first steps in this plane of existence. Yet, somehow, with love and compassion, you overcome and you go on to thrive. By the time you're in elementary school, it's almost as if that horrible beginning never happened. You're sitting around children who had a fairly run-of-the-mill entry into this world and there is no difference between any of you.

Giving yourself that same love and compassion now is what you need to do in order to move on from your past trauma – that which you can remember and which keeps you trapped in the glitch. You need to accept that what happened to you is not by any fault of your own. You need to recognize that you were present in that moment. You have lived through it and you do not need to live through it again. You cannot prevent it from happening again by obsessing over it and trying to understand it.

Now, let's look at another scenario where you're a little older and one where you didn't have the good fortune of being taken in by someone who could help you heal. You have grown up in this household with a drug-addicted parent and you have been exposed to substance abuse your entire life. Life will go one of two ways for you:

1. You will end up with substance abuse issues of your own.
2. You won't touch so much as a drop of alcohol in your life.

Which outcome do you think is better?

Any takers?

The answer is neither.

Yes, you read that right. Neither of these outcomes is better for you. Sure, one is going to be better for you in terms of your health, but you might experience just as much of a crippling mental health issue as the person who grows up to be an addict too. You are so traumatized by your past that you have purposefully stopped yourself from encountering anything remotely similar to the substances that your parent used. You have gone out of your way to make sure that you are the complete opposite of them, but in doing that you haven't necessarily found your true self. All you've done is ensured that you are not like them. That is a life lived in spite. You are doing everything "in spite" of your past not "despite" your past.

The third scenario has nothing to do with drugs at all. It is the far more sinister realm of emotional addiction. We say it's more sinister because, like the second person who grows up to be nothing like their drug-addicted parent, the trauma can be harder to track and, thus, harder to treat. You can't fight a glitch that you refuse to believe is there. "I'm nothing like my parents so I'm fine." That's the sentiment, right?

Wrong.

The reason why our identities get tied to our glitches is that, in part, we become more than accustomed to living our lives in the glitch. We become addicted to it. If things are going well for too long, we become suspicious and wait for the other shoe to drop. We find a way to bring the drama back into our lives and when it does, we tell ourselves that we were right to believe that this life of joy couldn't last. It's drama addiction and self-fulfilling prophecy in a dirty, twisted tango with unending music going in the background.

The only way to detach from this is to fully believe that you are not your past. Your identity needs to be rooted in your truest self and not in the past pain that you think has defined you up until this point in time.

You Are Not Your Past

We're going to keep going with the "drama addict" narrative. It's important for you to understand what we mean when we use that term. We're not necessarily referring to someone who finds themselves in petty arguments and fights more often than they should, although these people are dealing with a glitch of their own. No. What we're referring to at this present moment is the self-fulfilling prophecy that we just looked at. When a person has been exposed to "drama" for prolonged periods or the cycle has seemingly repeated itself throughout their lives, it can be painfully hard to break free from it. In essence, you begin to wonder who you are if you aren't in the midst of a battle, and this unknown reality – this peaceful place that you very seldom experience – begins to feel like the enemy. We'll get into the precise reasons for this in Chapter 13. For now, let's focus on the drama aspect of things.

Let's hypothesize again.

You were that little kid who grew up watching their parents fight and in a matter of months, you went from being frightened by this new behavior, which your parents were exhibiting, to normalizing and internalizing it – using anger and aggressive behavior as a defense mechanism. Your brain is built for survival and if it can see that the frightening behavior isn't going anywhere, it has to find a way to accept it for the time being and normalize it. In other words, this abhorrent behavior becomes the new normal for you. The behavior continues over the years and, soon enough, your brain no longer views it as abnormal behavior. You're in your teen years and even though your rational mind tells you that this isn't normal, your internal correlation with love, normalcy, and intimacy is fighting. You begin to rationalize the trauma and feel as though maybe everyone is like this in a relationship. Maybe your parents are just living a normal life and you're the one who is too sensitive. More importantly, you become so accustomed to this drama that your life feels strange and empty without it. You emit this homing beacon for drama in your life and you don't feel balanced until a fight of some sort – internally or externally with other people – has cropped up in your life.

This is no longer survival mode. This identity attachment to the glitch.

Now, this is not an opportunity for you to look at what you experienced as a child and automatically begin hating everyone who exposed you to certain things that they shouldn't have. Doing this is like swimming back upstream against a strong current with a torrential downpour coming in over your head. It is not going to work in your best interests and it is going to exhaust your emotional reserves. Plus, this is exactly what the glitch wants you to do. It wants you to keep looking back. It wants you to stumble as you take your first few steps into the healthy spiral. It wants you to fall and force your way back to the door so that you can recount every single bad thing that has happened in your life. It wants you to ask "why?"

Well, why not?

Why not you?

Why should it be anyone else other than you?

When you accept that these heinous things happen all the time to anyone, anywhere around the world and that you are really no different, you will become more accepting of your past. You do not need to condone or reject the behavior of others, no matter who they were in your life. Your parents were in their own glitch. The drunk driver that ran you off the road and nearly killed you was in their own glitch. People all have their own glitches. Trying to understand the trauma that was inflicted on you by someone else is virtually impossible. You will never understand why it happened or what could have happened differently because you don't have insight into their lives and how they processed their own trauma. All you have insight into is your own trauma and how you process it.

So, your goal should be to understand your glitch and not what someone else inflicted upon you. You should try to understand how you felt in the moment when the trauma happened. You should take the stance of viewing your past self and not the incident itself or the other parties in question.

Your focus has to shift from them to yourself.

You are not your trauma. It doesn't define you, nor did it make you stronger. It made you harder and more guarded. That isn't necessarily equated to strength. You are what makes yourself stronger and you don't need to hold onto the traits that you had to develop in order to navigate that phase of your life. You can wake up tomorrow and decide to be a completely different person and there is nothing that anyone could do to stop you. You, however, have to be willing to recognize the glitch for what it is.

Recognize to Release

There is a sense of peace in bringing to light what was once detached into the Unknown Other. This reabsorption is part of what we'll be discussing in Chapter 10 as we unpack the principles of JAMP© (AL-SAMARRAI, 2020) that can assist you on your journey. With this in mind, it's important to recognize the glitch in order to release it. When we're walking around with our eyes shut, it's easy for the elements around us – that are on the offensive – to swallow us up. In order to deflect the advances of the glitch, you need to see it as clearly as possible. When you can recognize that you're entering the glitch and pre-empt it, it will be easier to accept that you can exit it. You don't have to be swallowed up by it. But how do you do this? Simply put, it begins with a "small win." Your mind is so used to being overcome by the glitch that it has begun to believe that this is the way your life will always be. In fact, you might even tell yourself that you're never going to find happiness or peace and have come to accept that. While acceptance is a very important part of leading a life of contentment, this does not apply to accepting defeat. So, for you to move on from the glitch, you need to begin practicing the power of the small win. You can start by addressing one of your triggers that you are wholly aware of. This will attune your mind to pick up on the triggers that you are not always consciously aware of and, with practice, this process will become easier as time goes by.

Essentially, this can be regarded as a form of exposure therapy. However, with JAMP© (AL-SAMARRAI, 2020), we don't want to desensitize you, we want to short-circuit the complex altogether. When we run from our triggers, we are going to spend the rest of our lives running from them. Unfortunately, with trauma, a trigger can be something as simple as a change in the way a warm breeze hits your skin. It can be a certain time of day when you were repeatedly exposed to emotional neglect or abuse. You cannot run from a time of day. You cannot run from the changing of the seasons. To brave the meeting of your mind and the glitch, you need to ride out the immediate feeling of discomfort so that you can look it in the eye and reroute your reaction to being triggered. When you do this, and you realize that the glitch isn't as scary as it seemed, you will experience the high of a small win. This will assure you that you can tackle being triggered in the future and your mind will begin developing a pattern for how to react when triggered. This in itself will help you identify your triggers because you will be overcome by a similar feeling even when you aren't aware that you are being triggered. This will set off the alarm bells to make you aware of said trigger and you will become more self-aware. You can expose yourself and withstand the pain or you can dull your sympathetic nervous system using JAMP© (AL-SAMARRAI, 2020) techniques so that you can calmly reroute the negative energy swelling up inside yourself.

This is now our precursor to your threshold for discomfort, which we'll elaborate on in Chapter 13. When you're standing in that hula hoop of certainty and you're repeating these patterns that allow the glitch to keep you crying out in agony, you're not taking control over your threshold for discomfort. You're allowing something that happened in your past to exact pain on you. You have to be willing to up the ante on your emotional discomfort now so that you can progress into the spiral. You have to be willing to become refined by trial. The problem that many of us have is that we think that we're accustomed to the discomfort of the glitch and, therefore, would rather linger in this limbo than risk moving up the first step only to be thrust into a higher level of pain. But pain isn't an elevated experience. It remains on that living room floor as you learn to embrace the fire of life's refinery. The more it refines you and the more elevated you are off that living room floor, the more comfortable the pain of progress will become.

You have to be willing to risk the comfort zone of that hula hoop to stare the glitch down.

*

Part of detaching your identity from the glitch is reaffirming to yourself that you are not betraying yourself, or anyone else for that matter, by releasing it. If you're afraid of facing the glitch, it will beget more fear. If you are uncomfortable with tackling your past, you will always be its prisoner. You have to scratch the record to prevent the fracture in time from keeping you in a loop.

CHAPTER 6 – A FRACTURE IN TIME

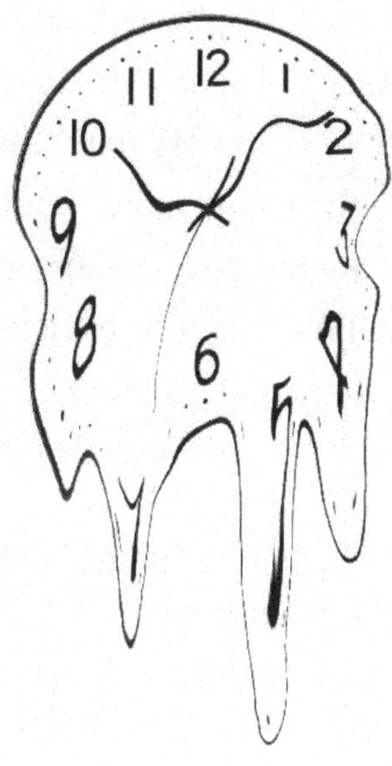

Time is a curious manmade invention. It marches on, as they say. It waits for no one and, yet, it can shift according to the mental state that we're in. If you find yourself in good company, an entire week can feel far too short. If you're stressed out, even five minutes can feel like an eternity. Part of activating time in a meaningful way comes from how you deal with the glitch and the reaction that it causes in your body as we'll come to discuss in *Muscle Memory*. This is where we will discuss how your physical self keeps the score of your trauma. At this juncture, let's dive into the physical activation of time and all its fractures.

Standing in your physical form and refusing to recede into your mind is the best way to stop the glitch from sending you back down memory lane. As you'll come to learn from *The Phantom Projection* and *The Glitch's Secret Weapon*, the glitch can't actually bring you back down to the trauma once you begin your climb into a higher vibrational frequency that is more in tune with your true Self. It can only project images and use trickery to make you think that you are still stuck with it. It's crafty and because it loves company, it's not going to let go of you that easily.

When you're able to placate your own discomfort in the moment that a trigger presents itself and you can do so without retreating into your mind, you will be able to override this trickery. You might physically tense up, lock your jaw, or grimace. This is your body's way of repeating the bodily movements that you most likely reacted with at the time that the initial trauma took place. We say initial trauma because the constant reliving of your past can retraumatize you.

This goes hand in hand with the internal mother or the mother complex. We have all of this love and patience within ourselves for others – love that can soothe a crying child or make a skinned knee feel less painful – but very little for ourselves. The glitch loves the busy person and the distracted person because when you have no time for yourself, you are always in fast-forward mode. And when you're in fast-forward mode, you're much like a new mother who is burnt out, exhausted, and running on fumes from having only had four hours of sleep. You're irritable and frustrated. More importantly, you don't have the time to identify a phantom projection for what it is. Everything feels like the end of the world when you don't take the time to slow your body down and sit still within this vessel.

This is partly why people will often tell you to sleep on decisions when you're feeling emotional. In those first few moments of daylight after you've slept on something, your body is far more at ease than what it was the night before. You're in this ethereal halfway point between the spiritual and physical realm, and you can wake up with picture-perfect clarity. That is unless you've sent your body into battle before you've slept. If you've had a little too much to drink or you've stayed up too late, your body is going to be working hard to make up for the exhaustion you've thrust upon right before bed. It, therefore, won't have the time to run through that hard reset where your muscles go through their restorative processes and your mind can set your spirit free momentarily as you enter rapid-eye-movement sleep.

Being able to sit still within your own body, breathe deeply, steady your heart rate, and mother yourself is how you prevent time from dragging on while your heart rate is soaring. After all, this is what happens when you're in constant survival mode. Your senses are heightened and everything can be perceived as a threat, yet time seems to stand still while your brain decides whether it needs to fight, flee, or freeze. At that precise moment, when you're worn down and ready to throw in the emotional towel, the glitch fires up the phantom projection.

The Phantom Projection

Remember that staircase that we looked at in Chapter 4? Well, the glitch will try to get smart on you. It will try to project the images along the outer rim of your hula hoop – the ones that it had used to catch your eye before. This is because the higher up the spiral staircase you climb, the further away from reliving the trauma you are. Since the glitch is a big bully that doesn't like stairs, it can't come up after you once you've reached a certain level of healing. All it can do is project those images and it will try to do this at your weakest moments. Those nights when you're exhausted from staying up to care for your newborn. The mornings that you feel like you can barely get out of bed because of the all-nighter you pulled. The moments after a heated disagreement with someone you care about. In all of those moments, you are going to be giving off a homing signal to the glitch. It's going to take this as an opportunity to project the trauma that once acted as your trigger. It is going to try to suck you back down the staircase.

You don't have to let it.

Furthermore, unless it was a completely life-altering argument, the glitch not going to be able to do this. The glitch just wants you to think that it can. The absolutely worst thing that you can do, when this happens, is fire up your rumination processes. Flashbacks are going to keep you trapped and you might feel like there isn't a way to stop them from coming, but there is. We've used the word contentment throughout the book and there is a very good reason for this. It's linked to the window and the trapdoor that we looked at earlier.

One of the predominant problems of our generation isn't that we are excessively downtrodden, but that we have this false belief that life is meant to be easy. When we encounter trauma, pain, and strife, we think that our lives have gone wrong. This in itself can become a part of our Shadow or Unknown Other that acts as a foot soldier for the glitch. We have to be of the mindset that life is hard. There isn't a single person on this earth who hasn't suffered some form of physical, emotional, and psychological pain. Life is not meant to be easy. When you accept this, and simply view the next hurdle in your life as a naturally occurring event, the glitch doesn't have the emotional fuel to send you into rumination. It doesn't have the power to trip you up on your journey and distract you from the staircase ahead or above. You give your trauma power when you are afraid of it and when you keep telling yourself that what happened was wrong. Yes, it was wrong and according to you and your indoctrination, someone always needs to pay the price when they've done something. Things need to be reconciled. Someone needs to be punished. The wrongdoer needs to acknowledge their slight and apologize. When you're of this mindset, the phantom projections keep coming. Every time you are angered, tired, stressed, or emotionally drained, you are going to take your thoughts back to these places. That drama addict in you is going to want to cast out more and more of this past pain, and all that does is make the Unknown Other bigger and bigger.

Imagine having entire pieces of yourself that you refuse to accept. Imagine wanting to cut off your right hand because you once made a mistake while you were writing. You cannot change the past. It didn't make you stronger. It doesn't have to define you. It is simply something that exists in the history of human existence – your human existence.

You need to let go in order to stop yourself from encountering the glitch's next secret weapon.

The Glitch's Secret Weapon

In this book, we explore how – once you're high enough on the spiral – the glitch cannot pull you back down the staircase. However, it does have a secret weapon in its bag of tricks and this is the fracture in time. When you have made progress on your healing and self-discovery journey, and you experience a trauma severe enough to cause a mental breach, the glitch will try to open a fracture in time alongside you. It will try to make you think that you are back at the bottom of the staircase. You will become so focused on staring out into this rip in the fabric of time that it will keep you stuck right there on that specific stair. You won't be sucked back down, but you won't be able to continue climbing either.

When this happens, the glitch can become so consuming that you replicate the patterns that led to the trauma in your past. With this, the glitch provides you with yet another hula hoop to ruminate on for the foreseeable future. Oh yes. It opens that rift in time up and you make the decisions that lead to the beginning of someone else's trauma or your own – a brand new trauma, for that fact. And this brings us back to the mother concept.

When we looked at the scenario of you projecting your past onto your children, this is the moment that we were leading you toward. As a parent, the more you try to push out those sides of yourself that view as undesirable, the more they will become present all around you. In a moment of exhaustion, frustration, or fear, it is highly possible for you to inflict the trauma that you are trying to get away from and to inflict it onto those that have come through the door behind you. As mentioned, the glitch wants you to believe that life is meant to be perfect and peaceful all of the time. It will have you feeling like you are inadequate and less than those around you, especially in this world of picture-perfect Instagram lives. As you strive for your version of perfection, you will lay waste to everything around you. Everything you touch will be tainted because you will not be acting and reacting from your truest self. You will be doing so in spite of the traits of the Unknown Other.

If your parents never showed up for any of your games, you'll show up to every single one and, perhaps, push your child into playing a sport that they no longer have an interest in. If your parents let you go out past a reasonable hour when you were younger and you felt that this led to some questionable behaviors, you will become helicopter to your own children and push them away. If ***this*** happened, you'll do ***that***. If **A** was the answer when you were a child, you'll make **B** the answer for your children. And so, on it goes.

Now, here's the antithesis to this concept: the glitch will do this even in the most beautiful moments of your life. You will sit there thinking that this is the most stressful moment in your life and miss out on all the joy because of your desire for perfection and your desire to shield yourself, as well as those you love, from the inevitability of pain. This will then manifest itself in your physical form.

Your body will keep tallying up your past pain and adding to it if you don't develop the awareness of this muscle memory.

Muscle Memory

Your body – your actual physical tissue – will hold onto your past. This is why you can relive your past pain so intensely because the original glitch has etched the pain into your flesh and fascia. More often than not, when you experience trauma, you operate from your hypothalamus which is, in simple terms, your instinct arena. Your body will tense up even if the threat is not physical and your body will hold onto that. The more trauma you experience, the more difficult it is to release the trauma from your body. There is both a physically scientific reason for this as well as a psychosomatic one. Physically, your fascia can become dehydrated and stiff when you go through any manner of trauma – physical or emotional. It is part of your body's response to stress hormones that are sent coursing through you at the time of your trauma. If this happens repetitively, your fascia never really has the time to recover before the next onslaught. As such, your body becomes accustomed to functioning in this state of rigidity. The other reason, which we've already discussed, is the physical manifestation of the mental recollection of your trauma. If you were physically attacked or hurt, your body can recall this pain even years after recovery. If you were emotionally traumatized, that tension can be relived in the flesh.

There are many physical therapies that can help you reengage with your physical self and unlock the rigidity in your fascia, ultimately setting you free from a physical prison that has been coupled with your mental prison. A few simple steps to bring yourself back from the realm of the Shadow and become more present in the moment include deep breathing techniques and mindfulness practices. Have a look at two prime examples below.

Deep Breathing to Unlock Your Fascia

When your body tenses up, your chest will tighten and your breathing will become shallow. All of the energy in your body will be diverted toward your senses as your stress responses kick in. When this happens, you need to stop and breathe. This is the only way to get back to your logical state of mind and to stop the trigger from making you act out based on the feelings in your body as you relive your trauma. Become completely aware of where the tension lies in your body and begin trying to loosen up these areas. If your jaw is clenched, yawn and stretch out your facial muscles. If your shoulders are curled in, roll them back and sit or stand up straight. Take a couple of deep breaths into your belly and, with each breath, hold the air in for a few seconds. Deliberately inhale, as if you're training your brain on how to breathe. Exhale through your nose and assess the situation for what it is.

If this is a natural waking state that you find yourself grappling with, try the following mindfulness practice in the morning.

Mindfulness to Pull You Out of Your Mind

You're going to begin by turning the shower on and standing outside the shower or tub while you watch the water cascade and listen to it gushing out of the shower head. This is the first activation of your senses. Thereafter, get in and stand under the water. Take note of everything from the temperature to the sensation of the water trickling down your skin. Accept that you are alive within this moment. There is nothing happening right now which is a threat to your existence within this moment. Watch as the beads of water roll down your body. You are at the helm of this experience. What lies beyond this bathroom is inconsequential to this very point in time. Analyze the scent of your soap or body wash. Ignite every sense and breathe as slowly and methodically as possible. This will bring you back to reality – away from the past and the future.

This will help you heal the fracture in time.

*

These fractures in time prevent you from living in the present moment. Even as your healing takes shape and you become more aware of your trauma, you need to develop the grit to analyze your feelings and stop your triggers from getting out of hand. If this doesn't take place, the trickery of your glitches will have you missing out on this experience that we call life. Your perception will play a pivotal role in how you are able to traverse this space.

CHAPTER 7 – CHANGE YOUR VIEW, CHANGE YOUR WORLD

The way you perceive the world is the way the world will be. The way you perceive your experiences and your life will manifest those very perceptions before your very eyes. In a little while, we're going to explore the experiential lens, but before we get there, let's address how you might have perceived the world and your experiences up until this point. As we discussed in accordance with the mother complex, the closer you are to your glitch, the more you will try to avoid anything remotely similar to it. So, when you're resisting the path that could lead you to become like your own parents and when everything that you do is an attempt to be the antithesis of your past, you're actually still fairly close to the glitch. The further you are away from it, the less likely you are to do things as a means of proving that you are not your attacker. Your attacker could be a person. It could be the trauma itself. It could be a past experience. Whatever it is, when you're trying to escape it without identifying and addressing it, you are probably still being held back by it.

Whether you're a parent or not, you may have already experienced a moment in your adult life when you've said, "Oh God! I sound like my mother/father." This realization that you have traits that are similar to your parents – perhaps parents whose parenting you have openly criticized in your adolescence – makes you want to run from this behavior. Instead of trying to understand what has sparked this behavior, your immediate reaction might be to remove this side of yourself and cast to the Unknown Other like scraps being thrown to a wolf. This is because of your perception of how life should be. You might think that becoming similar to your parents is a betrayal of your teen self who said you would never become like them. You might perceive yourself as having been wrong in your adolescence, and no one ever wants to be proved wrong, right? You might also see this as a sign that you are an inauthentic person who doesn't stand by the things that they've said. However, you're looking at the picture all wrong. If we held a toddler accountable for saying they would never speak to their sibling again, half the world wouldn't be talking to one another. You need to stop seeing your adult self – or even your adolescent self – as the permanent version of yourself. You are going to go through the fires of the refinery of life many times over. You cannot keep expecting to come out the same way.

Our point is this: you need to change the way you view yourself in relation to the world around you as well as in relation to your past self. Accept the little deaths that occur throughout your life and lay that part of yourself to rest so that you can be born anew as the person who needs to exist at that specific level of your elevation in healing.

Your perception will be projected onto the world around you. If you think someone is a certain way, you will base your interactions with them on that belief and they, in turn, will fulfill your perception of them. How does this relate to the glitch? We'll tell you how. When you perceive your past as something that needs to be changed via your actions today, you will expose yourself to everything that you already believe is wrong in the world. This is also known as the experiential lens.

The Experiential Lens

We're back in the living room – the one where you spotted someone exiting the room via a spiral staircase that led to a trapdoor in the ceiling. When we worked through this example there was a little breadcrumb that we left for you in terms of your perception. Do you remember what that was? If you can't remember, here's a recap. There were two perceptions that we looked at in that example:

1. Your perception of the cold, vastness of the universe beyond the window.
2. The other party's perception of the bright sunny day beyond the trapdoor.

Whatever you believe is real will be real. How far you've come away from your glitch will determine how you view the world and how you react to it. But how you view the world and react to it, will determine how far you can move away from experiencing a glitch. It's the quintessential catch-22. Jung said it best in Volume 6 of his collected works, Psychological Types. How objects appear to us is influenced as much by the physical aspects of the object as they are by our own intuitive senses and perception of the object. In other words, your mind imprints onto things that which it perceives them to be. If you look at someone and think that they are being secretively malicious, you will pick up on every undertone in their words and physical movements. You will project onto them that which you already believe even if it isn't really there. Now, this isn't to say that this person hasn't been malicious toward you in the past or that they won't act this way again in future. However, you will forever view your interactions with this person through the lens of past experiences – either with them or people like them. The most emotionally receptive people have the ability to see the archetypes in others. They have the foresight to link certain appearances, body types, behaviors, and mannerisms back to other people of a similar nature, who they may have encountered in the past. If you are one of those people, it can be difficult to shift your experiential lens because your intuition is always on. You're always receptive to unspoken words and hidden meanings all around you. While that isn't necessarily a bad thing, it has to be honed and your lens has to be adjusted so that your perception doesn't interfere with your daily life.

If you view life and death as something to be feared and endured, you are going to have a hard time letting go of your trauma. As we already mentioned, you cannot be of the mind that life is meant to be easy. For the most part, all forms of media are to blame for this narrative. We look at pictures of happy families on vacation and we think that they have it all. We feel that we don't have the right people in our lives or that we don't have enough money and, ultimately, we fantasize about having someone else's life. We don't what it took for them to get to a place where they can vacation with their family. We have no idea what pain hides behind those smiles. We only assume that everything is picture-perfect. We hear news stories about overnight successes and we think that this could never happen in our lives. We convince ourselves that they got lucky and then we idolize these people as if they were gods, simply because they have more currency to their names. We have no idea about the work that went into their success. We don't about the stories that they don't share – like the lonely kid who sat alone at lunch every day and whose ideas of inventions were their only company.

We see all of these "others" and we think that everyone on earth must have it better than we do. People in war-torn regions are pondered about momentarily, but we're totally apathetic about their plights. After all, we grew up in modernity where we had all of the amenities we could ever need, yet we're still no Musk or Bezos. Materialism and the idea that you have to have more to be more will crack your lens. It will smudge dirt all over it and it will have you searching for answers in your past. "Oh, I can't have **X**, because my childhood was like **Y**."

One of the few things stopping you from having the life that you long for is your perception. Your life is in your hands and your hands alone.

Your Life in Your Hands

When you heal and remove yourself from the cage of your past, you will see how different your experiences with everything around you will be. The world will literally change before your very eyes. We'll give you an example. If you've been taught that eating cheese is bad for you, both spiritually and physically, and you grew up in an area where this was a generally accepted belief, you are going to view people who eat cheese as debauchers. All of your interactions with the world and those around you will be shaped by this aversion to cheese and this belief that it is as good as sin. A friend will bring a cheesecake to a party and you'll lose your cool. You'll head out for hamburgers and a beer, only for the hostess to forget that you said "no cheese," and you'll get up and leave when a cheeseburger winds up in front of you. You will be completely of this belief that anything to do with cheese is going to be detrimental to your health and your peace. You're going to view people, places, food, and more through this cheese-hating lens, and everyone around you – well – they're going to be pretty confused. This applies to just about everything in life and we'll get to this a little later on under *The Tribe Illusion*. Who you were as a child and what you were taught to believe is simply luck of the draw. If you had grown up in the Congo, you might not have been provided with the same belief system as someone who was brought up in Brazil, or China, or Scotland. While your archetypal framework can't really be altered, your understanding of it and your belief system can. This is why we said that you are not your past.

We, as human beings, assign meaning to things. The first person to see the sky and call it blue could have called it anything else. They could have called it sock and we would all refer to the color that we know as blue by the name "sock." None of it has meaning and **all** of it does. You decide what that meaning is, not your teachers, your church leaders, your parents, your friends, your lovers, or your idols. It's just you. You have the power to decide what is important to you and what isn't. You have the privilege of deciding to create a world around you that feels more like home than home ever did and it all begins in your mind.

Just as the glitch can project images of horror, terror, and trauma, you can project images of wholeness, completeness, and contentment. The pursuit of your life should be the pursuit of balance, not happiness. Happiness is merely a byproduct of that balance and acceptance. It is a slow, comfortable oozing into a frequency that neither dips nor spikes erratically. It simply vibrates steadily and unwaveringly. You didn't come into this world to please anyone – to serve others when you can, sure, but not to please. Understanding that your life is in your hands and that you're not going to be sent to a timeout for making a decision that didn't go according to plan is one way to let the glitch know that you have given it all the energy that you can give. You're not going to keep it company anymore.

You are allowed to manifest your destiny just as you see fit and nobody needs to give you the thumbs up in order for you to do so.

Manifesting Your Destiny

The term "manifestation" might ring a bell for many of you. In recent years, this word has been thrown around, beaten over the head by pop culture, and used in the wrong context more times than we could care to count. Manifestation is not some type of trick that will get you a Lamborghini if you put that thought out into the universe. Manifestation is a process of projecting your thoughts and energy onto the world around you and aligning your actions to achieve that which you truly desire. Unfortunately, most people don't know what it actually is that they desire. A person might want a flashy car so that they can prove to people that they are somebody. This might stem from a childhood of feeling inadequate and a belief that material gain will get them the acknowledgment that they have always longed for. It's not the car they want, it's the acknowledgment. Someone else might want a boatload of money, not because they actually want the money, but what they believe it will do for them. This could be having more time to spend with loved ones or having the means to travel the world. Here's a news flash for you. There are people traveling the world every single day. There are people circumnavigating the world on their bicycles, crashing on sofas, and taking ferries as well as only a handful of flights to do this. There are people who are aligning their careers in order to spend more time with their loved ones or cutting back on the time that they spend on meaningless activities, like surfing the net, in order to get quality time. They know that quantity doesn't necessarily equal quality. It's all about perception and getting the most out of your day with what you have. There are so many souls on this earth who will never amass material wealth. Are they just supposed to mope around and keep hoping that they'll get it one day, or should they live in the only moment that it promised to them?

There is no tomorrow so beautiful that it is worth being miserable today. There is no past so painful that one can't find the beauty in the world around them. That was the whole point of the mindfulness practice. It was to make you more attuned to the present moment because tomorrow is promised to no one. It's not a cliché. It is a fact. Here is what we believe most people are pursuing when they think that they are pursuing happiness: wholeness. They are pursuing a place where they can feel completely at ease in their own skin, whether they're facing difficulty or not. They're pursuing that morning when you wake up and feel grateful for a new day. They are pursuing an existence that isn't plagued by constant pain. Yes, there will be discomfort and you should build up a tolerance for it, but you don't have to live in a constant state of agony. You don't have to let the past become the be-all-end-all of your life.

You are alive right now. You have purpose right now. You possess everything that you need to be the most balanced version of yourself. There is no mansion big enough to create the home within yourself that you desperately want.

*

As you begin to see that how you choose to respond to the world around you will alter the way that you see it, you will realize how powerful you are. Like a child who imagined vanquishing dragons in their backyard, you can create the energy around you that will drive you every day. You can see the rain as something gloomy or you can see it as the sustenance that both you and the earth need. You can see hardship as punishment or as an opportunity to grow. *The Power of Choice* is where it begins.

CHAPTER 8 – THE POWER OF CHOICE

You have the power to choose anything that you want in this life. The issue is that many of us are too scared to go beyond what has been holding us back. As we get older, the glitch isn't just some high school bully that we learn to get over. It turns into that narcissistic ex that keeps promising you to change their ways. It keeps you warm at night in the bed of familiarity until it ruins your day and sends you tumbling into despair for a week...or longer. You have to be willing to let go of it. This is why detaching your identity from the glitch is so important. When you're attached to it, you fool yourself into thinking that your past is a part of who you are. You go into preemptive mourning for the side of yourself that you think you're going to lose by letting go of the past. You become codependent – wrapped up in a toxic relationship with your past.

There is a saying by author, Laurie Buchanan, that speaks to this and it goes along these lines: "Whatever you are not changing, you are choosing." The reason why many of us have a difficult time making choices is not just because we are trapped in our comfort zone, but because we believe that we will be punished for one choice and rewarded for another. We think that universe doles out such things as punishment and rewards. What we fail to see, as per our last chapter, is that the universe only acts as a mirror for what is already inside you. If you order something from a new restaurant, and you are dissatisfied, you are not being punished for not sticking to what is tried and true. You are not being given a "that serves me right" moment. How you react to being dissatisfied with your meal is what will become the narrative in your head. You can either choose to see it as something that is not suited to your taste and try something else next time or you can allow the experience to force you back into your comfort zone where you will choose the same meal that you always choose, or opt for not ordering in so that you can avoid disappointment. This, as with every example we've given you this far, applies to life on the whole.

We make choices.

They have consequences.

That is all.

You are not being punished or rewarded. You took action and there was a reaction. Sometimes the outcome is good and sometimes it's bad, but you will learn something every time. Again, your relationship with choice comes down to whether or not you were given independence in your younger years. If you were told what to think and not how to think, then the chances are that you have a very poor relationship with choice. If, as you got older, you were berated for your choices and made to feel as though you always made the "wrong" decisions, you are going to punish yourself when things don't go as expected. The universe hasn't stepped in to become the parent that once controlled your every move. You have. You have taken on that inner critic and it is empowering your glitch and blocking your ability to move on from it.

It's important to remember that life is about how you respond to it.

It's How You Respond

Life isn't what happens to you but how you respond to it. Your experiences are very real and equally valid, but how you respond to them will make the world of difference. The goal should be to train your mind to identify a trigger. When you're triggered and unaware of the fact, it is incredibly difficult – nigh impossible, in fact – to stop yourself from reacting in the same manner that you always do. When you're able to stop and say, "Hmm. I've been here before. I felt horrible after I reacted that way. I'm not doing that this time," you're going to circumnavigate the glitch. There is something so freeing about allowing yourself the opportunity to see that you do have the power to react and respond to situations differently. When you do things the way that you always have because you've told yourself that it's all just a part of who you are, you are going to repeat the same year over and over again for the rest of your life. You are never going to experience the sheer joy of rediscovering sides of yourself that you thought had been burnt up long ago or finding new ways of being that you have never experienced before.

To understand this better, we're diving back into the realm of hypothesis.

It's 5 PM – peak rush hour. You're stuck in traffic and it's about 90 degrees outside. People are practically sitting on their horns and it's beginning to give you a headache. As you sit there, you realize that there's been an accident up ahead which is making traffic move a lot slower than usual. You could sit there and complain about how inefficient the emergency services are or you could be grateful for the fact that you hadn't left the office a little earlier today. You could have been in that pileup. You could be grateful for the fact that you live in a country where the emergency services arrive at an accident scene as quickly as possible and do everything in their power to stabilize the victims so that there is minimal chance of further complications en route to the nearest hospital. You could take the time to just be with yourself and your thoughts before getting home. In life, similar to this accident scene, sometimes there is nothing you can do to change the situation. All that you can do is make the best of the moment. How you train your brain to see certain situations will help you move through them without inflicting more pain on yourself. This can be translated to being triggered by a situation that is similar to your trauma.

If you're standing in line at the checkout of your local grocery store and you find yourself witnessing a disgruntled shopper who demands that more checkouts be opened or, at least, provisions for self-checkout, it could send you back to a time when someone in authority yelled at you or around you. This might make you feel triggered. You had been patiently waiting in line the entire time, but as soon as this person starts mouthing off, you decide that you don't have the time to hang around. You drop your basket right where you're standing and walk out. As you enter the parking lot, you're annoyed at the fact that the store hadn't just hurried up and responded to the person's request. You're annoyed at yourself for leaving the groceries that you clearly needed. You're ashamed that you left a basket full of food on the floor where the constrained staff will have to find it and put everything back for you. What you're not aware of is the fact that it wasn't the slow-moving line that irked you, it was the complaining shopper. It put you in the mental headspace of that little child who felt helpless in a room full of people that you only wished would have spoken up on your behalf.

An alternative to trying to escape your trigger might have been for you to speak up and say, "Hey, buddy. We're all tired and we're all waiting. Making a scene is not helping." Maybe someone else would have backed you up. Even if they didn't, you would have faced your trigger. If he turned to insult you, he probably would have been tossed out of the store and you still would have walked out with your groceries and sense of self-worth intact. This isn't the only way to approach a situation of this nature. After all, there are times when it would be best to breathe through your trigger and not address someone who seems unstable – for your safety and those of the people around you. Moreover, this would be classified as desensitization and JAMP© (AL-SAMARRAI, 2020) seeks to address the trauma without having to undergo the discomfort of this scenario.

The point is that how you respond will either help you set your true self free or it will keep you mentally as well as emotionally stuck.

Mentally vs. Emotionally Stuck

You can be physically free but emotionally stuck. If you're "performing" well on the surface, but you're drowning beneath it, you are still stuck in the glitch. You need to find a balance between physical, mental, and emotional freedom to really move forward. We've already addressed how trauma can live within your fascia and affect your physical self; however, we haven't discussed the core difference between being mentally and emotionally stuck. When you are mentally stuck, you might find yourself ruminating about the past and replaying the situation as your inner voice tries to stand up to the trauma. As your mind moves from thought to thought, you might find yourself eventually feeling like a fraud and deciding that you aren't as tough as you think you are. Alternatively, you might continue to fight these battles as if they are happening in the present. When you're emotionally stuck, you might not mentally recognize the trauma, yet you'll continue to exhibit behavior that tries to remove you from any situation that is similar to your trauma. It's important to note that you can be physically, mentally, or emotionally stuck – or a combination of the three.

As we've given you a few tools to help you tackle being physically and emotionally stuck, let's look at how you can stop rumination from persisting.

Putting an End to Ruminating

When you find yourself repeatedly coming back to a thought, there is always a reason within yourself for it. Those elements that we find so abhorrent and undesirable in others are usually linked to something within ourselves that we haven't understood or accepted. These elements end up in the Unknown Other and, as the Shadow grows, we project it onto everyone around us. The Unknown Other will stand in front of you and as you try to see the person you are interacting with, what you're really seeing is their traits streaming through the filter of the Unknown Other. The thoughts that repeat themselves in your mind are often linked to the most undesirable parts of ourselves that we have projected onto others. Therefore, it isn't farfetched to think that when you have these arguments within your own mind – you know, the ones where you know exactly what to say during an argument, but only after the argument has ended – you're really arguing with your own Shadow.

"Everything that irritates us about others can lead us to an understanding of ourselves." ~ Carl Jung

Every emotion that you feel is a reflection of yourself. It is not a reflection of the other person. Yes, they have said something or done something, but your preconditioning and experiences have determined how you feel about what they have said or done. To stop being mentally stuck, you need to see yourself when you begin this mental argument. You need to acknowledge that you are not a mind reader and are, therefore, not arguing against statements that the person might have made. You are challenging a side of yourself that you have not accepted. You are fighting a part of you that you don't see as a part of you but as a part of the Unknown Other. Why do you think there is a belief that people who are too similar can't possibly be on the same team? The phrase, we believe, is that there cannot be two bulls in one pen. It isn't our differences that aggravate us and trigger us, but the similarities that we wish weren't there.

Exercising Your Ability to Choose

Earlier in the chapter, we gave you an example of ordering in. Whether you're in a relationship or have been before, or even if you've had a roommate before, you'll know the familiar song and dance of, "What should we get for dinner?" One person says "anything," and then they're not happy with the food when it arrives. Either that, or the pair of you go back and forth for about an hour until you decide that it's too late to order in, so you just make a sandwich and grab a family-sized bag of chips out of the pantry. Dinner done! And you didn't even have to make a decision. But you did. You made the choice to allow this side of yourself, who can't make decisions, to take hold; you made the indirect choice not to order in, and you made the choice to have a sandwich instead. Whether you're consciously aware of your choices or not, you make choices almost every single second of the day. In fact, you make a decision every two to three seconds. That's the equivalent of about 2,000 decisions a day – depending on your sleep-wake cycle.

To detach yourself from the glitch, you need to begin exercising your ability to choose. It can be something as simple as deciding what to get for dinner or something as monumental as changing your career, whatever choice you can muster up the willpower to make is what you need to do. If not, you will talk yourself out of it. That's why the longer you take to make a decision, the more difficult it becomes. We're not saying that you should make decisions that you haven't thought through, but your intuition will guide you in terms of the risks involved. As long as you aren't making a decision in the heat of the moment, while you're in a euphoric or saddened state, you can trust yourself to make a decision that is right for you. Not right or wrong, in general, but right for your current circumstances.

Start small and build up your decision-making muscle with time. This will remove the feeling of helplessness that comes hand in hand with being sucked in by the glitch. Also, the more decisions that you make, the faster you'll realize that you can live with the outcome of those decisions. Making a decision that doesn't work out in your best interests only reaffirms your stuck position.

*

Believing that you have the power to choose a life on your own terms is liberating. Seeing your boss as no more than another human being who just so happens to employ you is freeing. You will no longer feel like your employer has control over your life. Being able to make decisions, regardless of what you perceive people in authority may think, will set you free. While we're not recommending that you break the law, we are saying that you need to see everyone around you as an equal and not some godlike person that is higher up on some imagined hierarchy. This way of viewing reality opens you up to exercising your power to choose. It will also give you the confidence to address undesirable elements of your own persona that you may have excommunicated from your true self. Releasing the shackles of feeling subservient or inferior to any living person also requires you to release the tribe illusion.

CHAPTER 9 – THE TRIBE ILLUSION

This is undoubtedly one of the trickiest roads to navigate. Walking out from under the veil of the tribal illusion is going to help you heal and give you the power to live a completely authentic life on your own terms. We see the same story unfold all the time. Someone has this feeling of obligation to the people who raised them and those that they grew up around. They feel as though walking away from their early conditioning is going to be some form of betrayal that they won't be able to live with. However, if you're leaving family gatherings or lunches with your friends feeling more drained than energized, it's time to step away from the tribe illusion. Here's the kicker: sometimes you feel completely revitalized after being around your family, yet they still have a way of sucking you back into unhealthy thought patterns that you wouldn't have allowed to filter in while on your own. Now, most of the time, people think that they have to cut their family off completely in order to remove the tribe illusion from the forefront of their minds and actions. This isn't the case. Yes, there are families that are incredibly toxic and, therefore, you have to walk away from them. That being said, the world is full of people in the glitch. Remember the living room scenario? Everyone is either in their cycle, entering their spiral, or enlightened. Sometimes cutting people out of your life is necessary, but sometimes doing that is just an unhealthy coping mechanism. Running from the glitch isn't going to resolve the glitch. You have to be able to face your triggers. You cannot run from them and hope that nobody else triggers you in the same fashion years down the line.

The tribe illusion is one of the toughest chinks in the chain to break because we confuse indoctrination and preconditioning with an evolution of self. We hold onto these things because they form the foundation of what we think we know about the world. If you were raised to believe that exploring the arts as a career is a meaningless pursuit, that is what you are going to believe. If you grew up and began enjoying this exploration, you are going to feel as though you are going against the grain. If you experience struggles, just as everyone does in their career, you are going to tell yourself that you were wrong to go against your family's teachings. You will beat yourself up and ask yourself why you didn't listen to them in the first place. This is a prime example of experiencing the trauma of what you felt were your personal gifts being sneered at. When you identify with this illusion, which was created by your tribe, you deflate your confidence in your own talents and develop feelings of being lost or derisory. You will find yourself in this dichotomy of what you were led to believe and what you feel to be your truth.

You have to break that family tie on a spiritual level to live and stand in your truth.

Family Matters

Are you really living as this new person you have become or are you too tied to your family history?

When you keep living through the memory of who you were and where you came from, you're robbing yourself of the present moment. Yes, family bonds – if healthy – are essential, but they should not define you and how you relate to the world. But none of us are impervious to the supposed warmth of the tribe illusion. Each one of us, whether we care to admit it or not, has been marked by what we learned in childhood as well as the environmental factors that were in play. There are many answers that can be found by questioning what you were exposed to in your younger years.

Whatever complexes have been created within you as a result of your experiences within the tribe illusion can grip you for the rest of your life. The problem with these complexes is that their energy cannot be destroyed and this is why you will feel the glitch in your body. You will feel your trauma in the form of compulsions and anxiety. You will feel this electricity coursing through you and sitting still with your own thoughts will feel painful. These complexes will transcend time. They will prevent you from moving on and elevating yourself. They will stop you in your tracks and you will react to being triggered in the very same manner that you had reacted as a child. This time, however, your mind will be so tired of living through this cycle that it will become irritable and angry. Instead of cowering, you might find that you are prone to emotional outbursts and fits of rage. We see this quite commonly with people who experienced covert trauma in childhood – where the parents age and forget all about the events that traumatized their child and are confused as to why their adult child now lashes out at them.

This is because the trauma and the events around them cannot be absorbed by the child's consciousness. It has fractured or splintered off from the consciousness altogether and embedded itself like shrapnel within these complexes. The complexes then grow around the shrapnel like some form of scar tissue and the longer the trauma remains unaddressed, the harder it is to dig it out. You cannot work through emotions and thoughts when the energy given off by the complexes has your sympathetic nervous system firing away. It's virtually impossible. What needs to happen, in order for you to address these complexes, is for your parasympathetic system to be activated while you process dysregulated and splintered parts of your past. Yes, exposing yourself to the trigger and showing yourself that you can face the fear associated without running away from it is important, but if you are still knee-deep in the glitch this might prove to be more difficult than you thought. If you can bio-hack your own nervous system to slow your heart rate and breathing while experiencing a trigger, it will be easier for you to reabsorb the memory and digest the shrapnel. The only way out is through. It cannot be excised from your memory. To do this is to push further mental matter out into the Unknown Other.

Now, this tribe illusion is not one that was imposed on you and you alone. Most of the time, the tribe illusion has been handed down from one generation to another and previous generations feel as though they turned out fine and, so, continue to perpetuate this cycle of generational trauma. There is also this misconception among some generations that as long as a child hasn't been hit, no abuse occurred. However, neglect, yelling, fighting, emotional manipulation, asking the child to take on a parental role, "playful" teasing, and narcissistic tendencies, among many others, can be deemed as abusive and can cause trauma. Whether these things were intentional or not is irrelevant. Remember, you cannot rectify anything in those that traumatized you. You cannot expect them to change or to acknowledge their faults. That is their journey, which you cannot control. What you can do is recognize generational trauma and divert this energy that keeps you from entering a positive upward spiral.

Generational Trauma

Some illnesses are noted as being hereditary, but it is not 100% guaranteed that, because your mother had a certain illness, you will too. Your mind is a powerful thing and when you program it to believe something, it will come to be. Whether the familial trauma is emotional or physical, don't take it on as some form of inheritance. Generational trauma is commonly centered around abuse or adverse childhood experiences (ACE) which are passed down from one generation to another. We've touched on this concept several times throughout the book, but we will now expand it in further detail and we'll be starting with a very important question.

Who is at risk of generational trauma?

- Anyone whose ancestors experienced war, natural disasters, widespread racism and segregation, and catastrophes of any kind.
- Anyone with parents who were abused.
- Anyone who grew up in a home with substance abusers.
- Anyone raised with harsh discipline which was incorrectly seen as the norm for their parents' generation.
- Anyone who was abandoned and who moved through the foster system.

This isn't a comprehensive list by any means. If we were to list out the entire list of those who are at risk of generational trauma, we might use up every page in this book. Even then, we might not have included every single possibility. This should give you a broad sense of what to look for in your own lineage. It's important to tackle trauma as early as possible, to avoid prolonged damage to your neural pathways. As mentioned, these complexes act like little nuclear reactors in your body and the energy that they give off can eat away at your nervous system. Just think about it from the perspective of a piece of machinery, such as a car.

A car can only go for so many miles before it stops running as smoothly as it once did when it was originally purchased. It's not about how old the car is but about how many miles it has on the odometer. A collectible car could be kept under a tarp for centuries, being passed down from generation to generation and, with a little care, it will start up and run. However, a new car that gets used on a daily basis to drive a long commute might not last a decade before it gives out. Your nervous system is the same. You cannot have this system in a charged-up state and running on high around the clock without the damage being felt.

What's interesting about this example is the idea of a car being kept safe under a tarp. For the most part, you cannot wrap yourself up in cotton wool and preserve yourself. You have to be out in the world, engaging with other human beings, from the moment that you are born. Now, when the trauma that you experience isn't digested and processed out of your system, it will affect your microglia. What are microglia? The simple answer is that microglia are responsible for the normal functioning of your central nervous system. Their dysfunction due to the energy overload caused by the complexes can lead to a reduced local response to infection and injury. The long and short of it: trauma will show up in the body as mental and physical health issues such as anxiety and autoinflammatory disorders. If these issues seem to plague people in your family line, there may be an ancient trauma that is responsible for it. When generational trauma is in play, your genetic and neural composition can be impacted from an early age. This is why we refer to this type of trauma as covert – because you will think that the way you respond to the world is normal. It isn't. It is predetermined by the generational trauma that you have been exposed to. The good news is that you can overcome generational trauma and remove yourself from the "norm" of your own tribe illusion.

Before you can do this, it is important to address this generational trauma and to recognize the Jungian archetypes that you might be running from.

Jungian Archetypes in the Flesh

If you've ever had a dream that you didn't quite understand or an intuitive feeling that you cannot decipher, there are two possibilities. The first, and more obvious, is that it is your mind's way of trying to process the trauma that you have been directly exposed to. The second is that you are recalling information in the collective unconscious – a concept that we need to unearth now.

The collective unconscious is made up of shared instincts, intuition, and archetypes. We share these unconscious elements of our spiritual and mental selves throughout this plane of existence and this explains why we can feel like we've been in a situation before, even if we haven't. It explains why we know what to do, almost instinctively, when we're in danger. This connection to the collective unconscious can be used to our own benefit or our own detriment. It all depends on how you engage with it.

When we experience trauma or a fallout from the tribe illusion, it can feel easier to turn our back on anything that reminds us of this past. We already know that running from one's past only leads to more trauma and a fixed position within the glitch. If you have had the intuition to move on from what is no longer serving you, the chances are that your intuitive sense is also very perceptive of people's archetypes. Even if this perceptiveness occurs on the unconscious level, you will run from anything that reminds you of those who inflicted trauma upon you or exposed you to it. Running from becoming like someone in your family will feed the Unknown Other. Running from being around this person will have you running from every other person who reminds you of their archetype. Not only will you view everyone through the shadow of the Unknown Other, but you'll categorize them as someone that you need to go up against or stay away from simply based on their archetype.

At this point, we can dive into these archetypes and which side of ourselves they belong to.

The Ego	**The Unknown Other**
The Great Mother	The Tyrannical Father
The Wise Old Man	The Trickster
The Animus	The Anima
Meaning	Absurdity

Centrality	Diffusion
Order	Chaos
Time	Eternity
Light	Darkness
Transformation	Rigidity
Opposition	Conjunction
Sacred	Profane

The Self rules all, but the Ego and the Unknown Other take center stage and become disjointed from the Self, fighting one another. The more trauma that is present in the form of complexes that haven't been processed, the more inflated each of these sides of yourself will become. In the power struggle for dominance and the move away from the true Self, an imbalance arises that fuels the drama addiction within your psyche. The Great Mother longs to guide you and care for you, but the Tyrannical Father wants to rule with an iron fist. Both sides of yourself are necessary. There must be light to balance the darkness. There are times when we must be sacredly silent and times when profanity is called for. Remember, we're not trying to decipher right from wrong. We are trying to balance you.

Are these the only archetypes in existence? No. There are countless archetypes and they present themselves at various stages of your life. The Hero might present itself when you are thrust into turmoil. The Eagle may present itself when you depart from the physical world. There is the Magician, the Lover, the King, and many These archetypes are only the common ones that might crop up as your Unknown Other becomes inflated. In fact, most of the archetypes listed above aren't archetypes on their own. They are opposite ends of the same archetype. The Anima and the Animus, for example, can be seen as the masculine and feminine polarities of one archetype. The point of this is for you to understand how patterns may repeat themselves in different people and how you might relate to them based on your own complexes.

*

With a clear understanding of trauma and how it presents itself, as well as a foundational understanding of the archetypes, we can continue our journey into the principles of JAMP© (AL-SAMARRAI, 2020). These techniques will alleviate the pain of trauma and help you move through any future trauma that could potentially find its way to you.

CHAPTER 10 – THE PRINCIPLES OF JAMP© (AL-SAMARRAI, 2020)

Chapter 10

This is going to be the turning point for you. We need you to believe that wholeheartedly because, as you know, what you believe will manifest itself. Before we begin exploring what JAMP© (AL-SAMARRAI, 2020) is and how you'll be able to identify and combat the hidden monster that is the glitch, we'll need to explore the Shadow – or Unknown Other – in further detail. In healing your trauma, it's important to embrace the Unknown Other so that it can be balanced. It is only there as a shadow form because your ego rejects it and it, therefore, gets projected as a shadow aside from who you are. This is part of the preconditioning that we have all received. We use the word preconditioning because, to be frank, using the word brainwashing might not go down as well. It can be a tough pill to swallow.

Let's look at this as subjectively as we can. When we grow up, we're told not to play outside when it's raining. Snow days are only romanticized because we get to stay home from school and, potentially, have snowball fights with the kids in the neighborhood. That is if you live in a state where it snows. We graze our knee and someone is bound to panic. We cry and we're told not to, even if it's a well-meaning, "Don't cry. It will be ok." We are taught that there is good and bad in this world and that only one is necessary for us to thrive. We must always wait for warmer weather and sunnier skies, and now we're back in that living room. We're straining our necks to see the sunny skies beyond the trapdoor, but we fail to see that what lies beyond the room is only a projection of how we view the world. The person on the spiral staircase might not even have seen the sunny skies that you saw, but if that's what your mind told you that you needed to see to realize there was an alternative to the fear beyond the window, that is what you would see.

This indoctrination into believing that there is good and bad is the issue. It is something that you need to unlearn so that you can see the Unknown Other for what it is – a side of yourself that is neither good nor bad. It just exists. It is your perception of these facets of yourself that paints them as bad or good and this is based on what you've been taught. Depending on where you are in the world, what you perceive as bad might not be as bad to someone across the globe.

This can then lead to trauma eating you alive as you fragment all these parts of yourself and inflate the Unknown Other, giving your glitch an ally and ammunition. To nip this in the bud, we can use JAMP© (AL-SAMARRAI, 2020).

What is JAMP© (AL-SAMARRAI, 2020)?

Jungian Advanced Motor Processing, or JAMP© (AL-SAMARRAI, 2020), is a therapeutic process that helps you – the individual who has all of these trauma-induced complexes – to identify the pattern of the complex. Trauma, in itself, is an archetype. It takes on this form of the hidden monster and to revisit the sensation of the trauma without understanding its patterns is to remain stuck in the glitch. JAMP© (AL-SAMARRAI, 2020) seeks to move the energy that is created by these complexes and reroute it toward transformation.

How does this happen?

If you'll recall our discussion about rapid-eye-movement sleep, or REM sleep, you'll remember how we said that this period of sleep is necessary for processing the events of the day and for restoring the body. JAMP© (AL-SAMARRAI, 2020) bio-hacks this

REM process, inducing it while in a wakeful state, in order to calm the nervous system down enough to address the complex without the traumatized individual feeling like it will implode and suck them into the abyss with it. JAMP© (AL-SAMARRAI, 2020), essentially, places you in a trance-like state so that we can work with your sympathetic nervous (fight-flight-flee response) while you're in a state that is most closely related to the activation of your parasympathetic nervous system (relaxation response). The more energy the complex has, the further offline all of your other systems will be. You will dissociate from everything and your body will feel like it is separate from you. Your emotions will be strangers. Your thoughts will be invaders. JAMP© (AL-SAMARRAI, 2020) takes this energy that the complex is sapping and pushes it back to where it should be.

Yes, it is worth working with a JAMP© (AL-SAMARRAI, 2020) Certified Transformational Coach, but you can use some of these techniques yourself. At home, you can try:

- Mindfulness;
- Deep meditation;
- Self-hypnosis;
- Yoga;
- Reconnecting with nature;
- Positive affirmations;
- Grounding.

Mindfulness is already something that we've touched base on, so let's look into the other modalities available to you at home.

Deep-Meditation

To conduct deep-meditation at home, it's crucial to do this at a time of day when you won't be disturbed. Get into comfortable clothing that won't restrict you or have you feeling uncomfortable during the process. Light, cotton clothing often works best. Now, follow the steps:

1. Sit or lie down somewhere quiet and comfortable.
2. Make sure that all devices are set to silent and that there isn't any unnatural ambient noise such as a TV.
3. Close your eyes and take a deep breath.
4. As you breathe, take note of the movement of your chest and abdomen.
5. Focus solely on your breathing – the feeling, movement, and sound caused by this normal bodily function.
6. Keep this rhythmic breathing going and take note of all of the sensations in your body. Do not judge them or embrace them. Just observe the sensations and let them flow through you.
7. Once you have scanned your body, turn your focus back to your breathing.
8. Rest in this state for a few minutes.
9. Open your eyes and take a moment to return to your wakeful senses.

Reconnecting With Nature

The spiral can be seen everywhere in nature and this can help bring you back to your most natural state before you enter your own positive upward spiral. This technique is fairly simple and only requires you to spend as much time in nature as possible. Being in nature has the ability to slow your heart rate, decrease your blood pressure, and give you feelings of hopefulness. When you take the time to marvel at the natural world, your stress response will be greatly reduced and you will feel less trapped.

Nature is freeing.

Nature is rejuvenating.

Positive Affirmations

JAMP© (AL-SAMARRAI, 2020) Positive affirmations can help you fill a very negative space, which is left as the complex is digested, with incredibly positive information. Reaffirming to yourself the strength and power that you have within yourself will form part of the necessary energy rerouting. Here are a few positive affirmations that you can use on a daily basis:

• I am not afraid.	• I am kindness.	• I am light.
• I am powerful.	• I am compassion.	• I am freedom.
• I am strong.	• I am beauty.	• I am liberation.
• I am brave.	• I am amazing.	• I am liberated.
• I am fearless.	• I am happiness.	• I am free.
• I am loved.	• I am presence.	• I am celebrated.
• I am worthy.	• I am awareness.	• I am impressive.
• I am love.	• I am peace.	• I am wonderful.
• I am enough.	• I am deserving.	• I am profound.
• I am safe.	• I am magnificent.	• I am laughter.
• I am whole.	• I am consciousness.	• I am boundless.
• I am healed.	• I am light.	• I am connected.

Grounding

Grounding is another simple technique that you can do right now. Kick your shoes off and head outdoors. If you live in a home with a backyard, you can walk around barefoot on the grass. If you live in an apartment building, you can walk around your apartment barefoot or head to a clean, local park to walk barefoot on the grass. If you live near a beach, take full advantage of this. Walking on a variety of surfaces from the grassy boundaries of the beach to the soft, warm beach sand itself, and then to sturdier, smooth wet sand will work wonders for your mental, spiritual, and physical systems.

It's important to note that these techniques will help alleviate the symptoms of trauma. We encourage you to seek JAMP© (AL-SAMARRAI, 2020) treatment so that you can stop the symptoms from rearing their heads. Self-hypnosis and yoga are best explored with a practitioner before you attempt to practice on your own. These centering techniques will help you address the hidden monster.

The Hidden Monster Says Another Time

One of the core reasons why trauma can swallow you whole without you even knowing what is swallowing you is that it acts like a hidden monster. Sometimes, you won't even realize it's happening. This monster makes you disengaged because the trauma it represents is dissociated from you, yet controlling you. The monster will have you canceling plans. It will have you feeling ill, anxious, and unwell. It will do this to rob you of your freedom and once you cancel those plans, you'll feel miraculously better. This is how it controls you. It tricks you into thinking that relinquishing your freedom makes you happy and healed, yet it's just keeping you captive.

While there are people who are truly introverted, many people often confuse the hidden monster's tactics with introversion. An introvert truly does enjoy spending time with themselves, but they aren't necessarily afraid of being with other people. They simply value their alone time more.

If you get anxious every time your phone rings and you avoid calls altogether, you aren't introverted. If you're afraid of being in social settings, you aren't introverted. You can be an introvert and feel these emotions, but the two aren't synonymous with one another. Telling yourself that you prefer to stay in, only to scroll longingly through photos of your friends and family having a good time without you, this isn't a case of being an introvert. An introvert wouldn't long to be with others, yet feel too anxious to see them. Yes, introverts are selective with who has access to them, but they aren't anxious to spend time with those people.

Let's go back to the phone call issue. It would be worthwhile to take note of when you feel most triggered by a phone call. In most cases, anxiety in the body is usually linked to past trauma of a similar nature. However, you might not have been traumatized by a phone call. What you might be experiencing is trauma being relived in the body at a certain time of day and, thus, you feel anxious about engaging with people at that specific time of day. Also, take note of the people whose calls you often reject or ignore. In some cases, this can give you insight into how your glitch is making you relate to those people.

Are you ashamed of the way you're feeling and you're purposefully avoiding your friends because you don't want them to know? If so, is this the reason why you're avoiding their calls? Getting down to the root of what all of this means is going to give you insight, which you can use in treatment. If you're avoiding people who care about you, there could be a number of reasons for this:

- You don't think they'll understand your plight.
- You're afraid to appear weak.
- You don't want to be a burden.
- You have been the logical friend of the group and don't want them to view you in a different light.
- You don't trust your friends – or anyone else for that matter.

Here's how the hidden monster works in that regard. If you were traumatized in childhood, your fear may have turned into anger as a defense mechanism. You may have subdued your sadness by telling yourself to be strong – crying is weak. As you got older, you rejected this side of yourself and it was cast into the Unknown Other. Due to the fact that you think your emotional state is weak, you believe that others will look at your emotional state that way too. You judge yourself and, therefore, feel judged by others. What you view negatively in others is a reflection of your own perceptions. How you judge others is a reflection of how you judge yourself. Perhaps this isn't related to your friends, if you view them as equals, but someone in a traditional figure of authority.

Are you bothered by someone in particular? If so, who is this person and why do their calls bother you? You might, for example, be able to spend hours speaking with your own mother on the phone, but cannot stand more than five minutes on a call with your mother-in-law. Do you feel judged by her? Do you feel like she always finds a way to lead you into conversations that make you feel inadequate as a wife or daughter-in-law? Understand that she is in her own glitch. She is projecting harmful things upon you due to her own complexes. How you react to her is related to your complexes. You might have felt inadequate as a child due to the words and actions of someone else in authority. As such, you don't know how to respectfully stand your ground and deflect what your mother-in-law is projecting on you. Words turn into weapons and weapons embed this shrapnel within your complexes.

This is how you end up in a cycle of declining invitations, ignoring calls, and swiping texts away. The hidden monster pretends to be your ally and turns you against everyone around you. Whether their intentions are pure or not doesn't matter to that monster. All that matters is that you take on more and more trauma. All it wants is for you to isolate yourself and continue to project your own feelings of insecurity onto the words of others. It wants you to read between the lines, but not in a way that is guided by intuition.

JAMP© (AL-SAMARRAI, 2020) is the best tool to go up against the glitch and stop the monster from keeping you stuck in it.

*

JAMP© (AL-SAMARRAI, 2020) is an amazing tool that uses the Jungian map of the psyche to help redirect energy out of your trauma complexes and back toward your mind, body, and spirit. It will assist you in letting go of the self-judgment that keeps you in the embrace of the hidden monster and, thus, within the glitch. We can now unpack how the monster will try to become more covert once you begin your JAMP© (AL-SAMARRAI, 2020) treatment.

CHAPTER 11 – THE MONSTER'S AGENDA

JAMP© (AL-SAMARRAI, 2020) is a treatment that can produce results in a relatively short space of time. However, in that time, the monster that keeps you company when you're in the glitch will have its own agenda. The glitch is a mental space that you enter whenever you relive your trauma in the physical form and it cannot follow you as you move up your positive spiral. The monster which keeps you company, on the other hand, becomes even more covert as it begins to realize that its days are numbered. It will create false narratives in your mind that keep you in a holding pattern. Our goal, with JAMP© (AL-SAMARRAI, 2020), is to take the feelings that are felt in the glitch and turn them into emotions. When the energy moves into the emotional state, it can be processed as a thought. Once it becomes a thought, it can be transformed into a symbol. This can then be integrated back into the psyche.

The monster can no longer thrive in your glitch because, once the energy is moved, the use of positive affirmations disarms the defense mechanisms used by the complex. The monster, in essence, is the conflictual pattern that you hold within yourself as a result of the complex. The trauma, therefore, creates a complex which contains a conflictual pattern and your return to this pattern is what we have referred to as the glitch. These elements all take on a life of their own.

As we have already discussed all of these elements of the trauma archetype, it's time for you to embark on your hero's journey. The very first step of this journey involves your ability to identify the false hero.

The False Hero

As mentioned, the monster actually wants to be the hero of your story. It wants to prevent you from connecting with others. When it does this, and wins, it gets stronger. Before you know it, you've lost all contact with people that you care about – including yourself. The monster is lonely, jealous, and possessive. It wants you all to itself.

When you begin your healing journey, it is going to be difficult for you to decipher between the false hero and your hero archetype. Lines will get crossed and the false hero will have you thinking that it is a part of yourself that is working in a protective manner. So, let's go back to the mother-in-law example that we used earlier. While we never recommend trying to predict what someone else is thinking or feeling, we will use this example to show you how the monster can act as a false hero.

Your mother-in-law grew up in a large family. They were all quite close and she often felt that they were her greatest source of strength when she was a young woman. Before the birth of her first child, she lost both her parents and felt incredibly alone. Her own in-laws were of little help to her and she often thought that she wouldn't be able to make it along this new journey of motherhood without her own parents to turn to. Now that she is older and has overcome everything that she thought would tear her down, she has the great fortune of being present in her own grandchildren's lives. She often calls you because she is trying to remedy the trauma of being a young mother without parental guidance. She doesn't take into consideration that you have your own way of parenting. She doesn't think of the fact that you are fortunate to have your own mother around to turn to for advice.

She only sees her pain and, as she keeps entering her own glitch, she keeps coming back to this place of being lost and alone. She is now projecting that onto you and because we all operate from our own glitches, you see it as judgment. Perhaps you were always scolded for making mistakes as a child and now you find yourself seeking an image of perfection. She sees it as being helpful. Neither of you is right or wrong. You're both stuck in your respective glitches.

How does the monster fit into this context as the false hero?

The monster will tell you that ignoring her calls and avoiding her presence is your way of protecting your peace. This works completely counterintuitively because your life will soon revolve around minimizing your interaction with her. Unless she is outright malicious and narcissistic, you are preventing yourself from potentially having a wonderful relationship with another human being. This is, of course, based on a surface hypothesis. It doesn't factor in whether or not she was a toxic mother to your spouse or her approach when she addresses you. However, the most important facet of this interaction is your reaction. You cannot change her, control her, prevent her from trying to call you or help her recognize her own glitch. Your work lies with you. Even if a deep relationship is not something that you believe is possible with this person, you still have to do the work to not be so triggered by them. We'll say it again: if you spend your life running from your trauma, you are going to make a job out of it. It will become an unpaid career and it will eat up all of your time and energy on this earth.

We'll reiterate that you shouldn't attempt to understand the inner workings of everyone around you. This can be a slippery slope into the perspective vs. prophecy puzzle. You will believe that you know what people are thinking of you and, most of the time, those supposed thoughts will be negative.

This will, inevitably, happen as you isolate yourself.

Perspective vs. Prophecy

Once you pull away from people, you start to run these narratives of what you think they are thinking about you. You begin to feel isolated and make up these stories of what people are doing or saying about you. Eventually, you become so cold and detached that this acts as a self-fulfilling prophecy in the long run.

If you don't believe that this is possible, try this scenario on for size.

You're sound asleep and dreaming of something fantastical. All of a sudden, your significant other enters the dream realm. They are aloof and uncharacteristically cold toward you. Your mind immediately goes to the worst-case scenario: they're having an affair. Your mind fulfills this prophecy in your dreamscape because it's a narrative that it wants to explore. It isn't long before you spot them canoodling with another person. You knew it! You knew they were a no-good, lying cheater! You wake up in a cold sweat. Your significant other is still asleep beside you. You scowl as you look at their peaceful form, wondering what sinister thing they're dreaming about. In those few moments after your dream, you're convinced that what you dreamt was real. You feel distrusting and your energy just feels "off." You're hurt by this escapade that was manufactured within your own mind.

This is exactly what happens in wakeful reality when you isolate yourself from people. You can manifest the narratives that you have manufactured in your mind. If you feel like your friends are secretly judging you and you distance yourself from them, they might begin speaking about you out of concern. One of them might approach you and say something like, "(X) and I were speaking about you the other day. We're a bit worried about how distant you've been lately." All systems shut down. All you heard was "(X) and I were speaking about you." You start to think that they're secretly judging you and, a few days later, you exit the group chat that you've all been in for more than three years. This leads to them feeling as if they've overstepped a boundary – maybe they aren't as close to you as they thought they were. They, in turn, become distant in a bid to protect their own emotional states. You take this distance and the fact that they haven't come after you as if you were some kind of damsel in distress, as confirmation of what the monster had you thinking all along. The monster steps in as the false hero that has saved you from these merciless, venomous frenemies and it has won.

Your perspective or perception of the situation has led you to believe that you are prophetic. The false alarm bells that the monster will continue to set off will keep you repeating this pattern of isolating yourself from people. You will start to feel like everyone is out to get you and your trust meter will officially stop working.

This cycle will become a holding pattern.

Holding Patterns

We would like to reintroduce a side of trauma that we have not explored in detail up until this point. It is one that will either result in a complete rebirth or a holding pattern. This is the trauma of loss. For the purpose of explaining the holding pattern, we are going to look at loss in human form.

Let's suppose that you were exposed to generational trauma as a child. Your grandparents had survived a terrible catastrophe – for argument's sake, we'll say it was a war. They learned how to survive, but when they had actually escaped the clutches of war, they didn't know how to thrive. They were tense and constantly on edge as a result of post-traumatic stress and this often manifested itself in the way that they treated their child – your mother. Your mother was raised, along with five siblings, in a rural setting where everyone stayed out of everyone else's business – or so it seemed. Everyone talked about the abuse that was going on in your mother's parental home, but nobody did anything about it. Due to the fact that your mother was exposed to this abuse from such a young age, it affected the physical makeup of her brain. Her cognitive functioning was impaired and she struggled to pay attention in school.

As she grew older, she decided that her lack of focus in school was a sign that she wasn't cut out for academics and she married her high school sweetheart. That relationship was riddled with problems from the very beginning as they were both traumatized individuals who were codependently clinging to one another like proverbial life rafts. Soon after they wed, your father was offered a job in another state. It would allow him to provide a good living for you and your mother, and it also meant that she could stay home to raise you.

Being away from her family was the most freeing experience that she had ever had in her young life and she was beginning to enjoy being at home with you and raising you. A year later, your younger brother was conceived. He was born healthy and remained that way until he was 6 months old – when he started experiencing periodic fevers. Your mother experienced a great deal of trauma as she went from enjoying her time raising you to feeling as though she was stuck at home with a demanding toddler and sickly baby. While this was no fault of your own, she receded into past trauma and found herself continuously entering the glitch of the abuse she endured at the hands of her own parents. The situation that she found herself in would rattle even the most enlightened and healed person, but she had unhealed trauma on top of it all.

Months of going back and forth with doctors would result in the demise of your parents' marriage, only they didn't get divorced. They clung to one another in their codependency and, in so doing, traumatized you. Fights became the norm. Your mother would yell at you and spank you every time your playfulness woke your baby brother from his nap. Your life was lived in survival mode from a very early age, just as hers was. In their despair, neither of your parents realized what they were doing to you, or your brother, who was equally as exposed to the trauma.

As you grew older, you decided that you would pursue academics as a means of escape. Your books were your only solace and you eventually made it out of the household. Similar to your mother, you experienced trauma very early on in your adult life and found yourself in the glitch. You spent months holed up in your bed, feeling as though everything around you was just a different shade of gray – no matter how bright the day was. You want out and you've found JAMP© (AL-SAMARRAI, 2020).

You see, these holding patterns will repeat themselves in your life and the lives of those who follow you, whether they're your own children or your brother's children. They will continue to keep you in this traumatized state. You can spend years in therapy or you can commit yourself to 12 sessions of JAMP© (AL-SAMARRAI, 2020) treatment. JAMP© (AL-SAMARRAI, 2020) will allow you to release the pattern from the complex – that monster – and integrate it into memory.

*

This is the monster's agenda. It waits until the most opportune moment to use all of the ammunition it has been building up over the years. When you are triggered by something or traumatized once again, the whole world will feel like it's crumbling around you. You might even end up worse off than before because you will be dealing with double the feelings without being able to take them into an emotional state and then process them into thoughts. You will be stuck in a holding pattern. You will become a stranger to yourself and your vision, of the mental and spiritual kind, will become impaired.

To break free, you need to see yourself.

CHAPTER 12 – SEEING YOURSELF

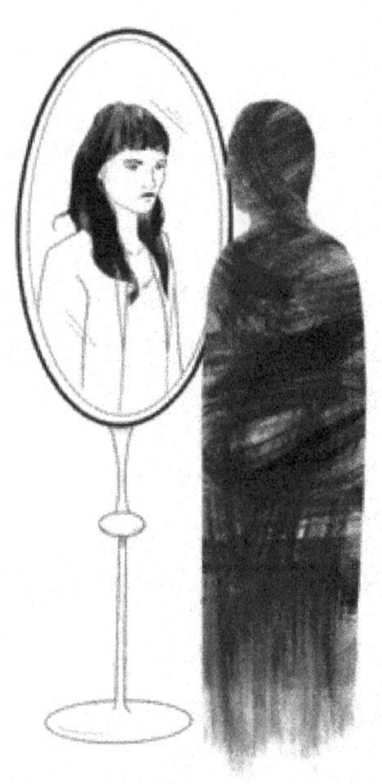

Do you see yourself? When you look in the mirror, do you see the person that you perceive yourself to be? We'll let you in on something – the person that you see in the mirror has little to do with your physical appearance. As you move into your healing and develop a mellow contentment for life, you will begin to see that the imperfections, which you thought you had, aren't as visible as before. This is because we hold trauma in the body and we project this tiredness as well as a defeated look into the mirror. What we're actually seeing in the mirror when we're stuck in the glitch is the fight between the Ego and the Unknown Other. You're seeing the archetypal energy of what is most prevalent in your psyche at that point in time.

You could be seeing the archetype that is your trauma as well. You could also see hints of the Sage, Innocent, Caregiver, Explorer, Hero, Ruler, Creator, Magician, Orphan, Lover, Jester, or the Rebel. You could be seeing the antithesis or the polar opposite to any of these archetypes. Mirror work can be used as a step into self-awareness and individuation. This is because the mirror, in symbolism, can have shamanic properties to it. It allows us a small window into the soul and can help redefine the way that we see others and what we project onto them. This, in turn, can help us see ourselves better and with less judgment.

It's vital to do this during your treatment because to forego this process is to become trapped in the oppositional side of the mirror while the Unknown Other takes more precedence. Mirror work can ease back this issue which is often caused by intentional mirror-gazing. What is that, exactly? Well, when we look into a mirror, we do so with intention. We do it when we're brushing our teeth. We do it when we're picking at a spot on our faces. We do it when we're combing our hair or fixing our appearance. The mirror, therefore, becomes a tool for the persona and for exacting the appearance that we want the world to see. We miss out on the opportunity to see ourselves as we truly are and, for many people, looking in the mirror for longer than necessary can actually be an uncomfortable undertaking.

To remaster the energy that is being spun by your complexes, you can use mirror work to stop the projection and, instead, feed yourself with positivity via the mirror before you. Before we provide you with steps that you can take at home, let's look at the shrinking effect.

Shrinking Violets

Yes, that's shrinking - not shrieking - violets. When you're stuck in the glitch, your body will contort to relive your trauma. We know that entering the glitch can cause facia rigidity and chronic pain, but it can also alter your physical form and, thus, the archetype associated with it. You could be 7 feet tall and still feel unseen due to the trauma that affected you once upon a time. You could shrink into an almost impossible stature because this is the physical structuring that is associated with your complex. You will literally shrink yourself into this past experience. There are four common reasons for this:

1. You don't want to appear weak and try to take up as little emotional space as possible. This translates to shrinking in your physical form.
2. You recoil into your frame because you are constantly on guard, waiting for the next attack.
3. Your confidence has been almost completely eroded and you don't want to be noticed.

4. Your trauma has physically affected how you carry yourself.

You might experience one or a combination of the aforementioned reasons and this will inhibit your ability to see yourself. You'll live in this almost imploded state where you feel that your physical form would collapse in on itself if it weren't for your bone structure being in place. As you look in the mirror, you won't be able to recognize the person that you feel you are beneath the layers of this invisible prison.

Looking at yourself in the mirror is, therefore, just the external adaptation of seeing your true Self – the one who has lost the ability to enact order between the Ego and the Unknown Other. Looking at yourself becomes uncomfortable because you are a physical, emotional, and spiritual stranger to yourself. Using the positive affirmations that we provided in Chapter 10; you begin your mirror work.

Mirror Work to Heal the Psyche-Physical Connection

The purpose of this exercise is twofold. It will show you where you hold resistance and it will help you remedy that resistance with time. If you look in the mirror and say, "I love you," or "I am love," and you immediately notice resistance in your body, you are not loving yourself at that moment. If you look in the mirror and say, "I am powerful," and you recoil as soon as you utter those words, you are not standing in your power. If, when you look in the mirror and say, "I am strong," you tense up, you are not in alignment with your strength. These are the areas that you need to address. You might not have felt loved in your childhood. You might have felt weak and afraid as a result of the trauma that you encountered. As you've continued to feed into this narrative, it has become a fallacy that has overwhelmed your truth.

If you can attempt to undergo mirror work every morning, we would highly recommend doing this. All you have to do is look at yourself in the mirror and repeat your affirmations. Within a relatively short period of time, you will begin to believe these statements and you will no longer cringe when you repeat them to yourself.

As we've already discussed, you will have to be willing to go through some form of temporary discomfort to break away from the holding pattern of the glitch.

Difficult Positions

Here's a question for you. Are you willing to go through temporary discomfort in order to shift the glitch? You've already gone through weeks, months, or years of living in this confined state, so taking the next step shouldn't be as frightening as it is. But it is frightening and we commend you for making it this far through the book. You might have already had some form of mental breakthrough or have been provided with insight into your trauma. This can be a painful reality to face.

Now, you need to retrain your body and your mind to acknowledge the trauma and how it's affecting your gait as well as your psyche. That is how you can begin moving past it. Making the trauma present can be uncomfortable but it is necessary. Meditating to release anxious energy can help, but it is like letting the steam out of a pressure cooker while keeping it in cook mode. You are going to have to continuously release that pressure because the problem is inside the pressure cooker. To switch the pressure cooker off, you can use your meditative state to work through the underlying trauma which has caused the anxious feelings in the first place. Again, we recommend getting in touch with a JAMP© (AL-SAMARRAI, 2020) practitioner to help you work through this, but you can begin doing some of the legwork at home.

Use the meditation that we provided earlier to uncover the underlying trauma that is plaguing you with anxiety. This is easier said than done because you will, most likely, experience these feelings when you're in a location that isn't conducive to meditation, which is why we always advise signing up for 12 JAMP© (AL-SAMARRAI, 2020) sessions.

Nevertheless, you can try the steps below if anxiety strikes when you're in a location that is suitable for meditation.

1. When your anxiety peaks, immediately find somewhere comfortable to lie down.
2. Close your eyes and listen to the sound of your breathing. Breathe in to the count of four. Hold your breath to the count of four. Breathe out to the count of four. Hold your breath to the count of four.
3. As you get into a rhythmic box-breathing pattern, assess the feeling in your body.
4. What were you doing right before the feeling set in? Is there anything about an upcoming event that is making you anxious? If so, why? Can you remember the first time you experienced this feeling? How about the last time you experienced it? What do you believe this is tied to?

5. As your awareness of the underlying trauma becomes more apparent, begin repeating the affirmations:
    a. I am safe.
    b. This is no longer my reality.
    c. I stand in my truth and I am whole.
    d. I am centered and secure.

You can repeat this meditative practice whenever uncomfortable feelings come up. Discovering your archetype in the moment will guide you toward deeper insight into your manner of retaining trauma and healing.

Archetypal Discovery

We've gone over a handful of the plethora of Jungian archetypes, but we haven't addressed how these might take shape within you. It is possible to have a dominant archetype as part of your true Self as well as several other archetypes that go to war with one another. Trauma, as discussed, is an archetype itself – and one that, generally, doesn't play well with others. We can say that it's an archetype because of the fact that it is an event that is recurrent across the human race. In other words, so many people experience similar trauma across the globe. Like love and music, trauma is a universal language that is embedded in the collective unconscious.

The Innocent - This archetype is common in childhood but it can transcend this period of your life. It is common among adults who have/had narcissistic parents. The child remains innocent and shielded as the parent controls everything, but as they grow up, they don't know how to trust their own instinct. Instead, they become too trusting of others.

The Orphan – People who have been made to feel like an outsider tend to possess the archetype of the orphan. If their parents showed favoritism toward a sibling, they may experience a strong urge to belong. They tend to be realists, but this can make them cynical at times.

The Hero – People who are in the midst of breaking the bonds of generational trauma and who seek belonging can be seen as possessing the hero archetype. In a hero's journey, there may be a battle between the peacemaker and the fighter as the hero learns when to fight and when to keep the peace.

The Caregiver – People who tend to sacrifice their own well-being for the sake of others can be seen as caregivers. This person may struggle to care for themselves as they step into the role of the martyr. They are compassionate, but might not show the same compassion to themselves. People who have had to care for younger siblings when they, themselves, were young might possess this archetype.

The Explorer – People who have felt trapped in their surroundings might possess the explorer archetype. As their minds wandered to escape their circumstances, they dreamed of traveling to distant lands and meeting new people. It can be hard for this person to be content right where they are.

The Rebel – People who come from homes that are rooted in generational trauma, which is tied to marginalization, may possess the rebel archetype. They want to break the status quo and they have a wild, free spirit. They might have encountered problems with authority or with the law in the past.

The Lover – If this person's parents made them feel as though they were only worthy of love when parental rules were being followed, they might possess the lover archetype. While this person comes off as loving and caring, they could be doing this to their own detriment as they constantly try to please others. They are, however, an incredibly reliable friend and partner.

The Creator – Again, if this person was exposed to the idea that they could not make mistakes, they might have taken on more of the creator archetype. They could be struggling with perfectionism in adulthood. Although they have so many ideas that they want to bring to life, their perfectionism leads to procrastination.

The Jester – This person has learned to deflect their emotions with humor. They very seldom lose their temper and some might view them as happy-go-lucky people. Beneath the surface, they could be struggling with the feeling that they are wasting time by not taking things seriously.

The Sage – The Sage possesses great wisdom and can often be referred to as an old soul. Exposure to trauma of all varieties might have prompted this person to grow up far sooner than they should have. As wise as they can be, their advice is often doled out to others while they don't follow it themselves. This can lead them to a life of inaction.

The Magician – This person is the transformational person in their lineage. They have the power to craft win-win situations where only conflict can be seen. They have attributes of the sage, but their ability to manipulate things to their will – using their foresight – can make them egotistical.

The Ruler – The ruler seeks to uplift their followers. They bring a great deal of prosperity with them and have excellent leadership skills. However, this person can often turn into a strong authoritarian figure that disregards the opinions of others. As such, they might struggle with maintaining relationships.

*

Understanding trauma's influence on the archetypes that you possess will allow you to cultivate a mental space where you're more aware of why you possess certain qualities. It will also give you the tools to uncover some of the negative traits that are associated with your dominant archetype. Once you do this, you'll need to assess whether or not you're living within the realm of comfortable pain.

CHAPTER 13 – COMFORTABLE PAIN

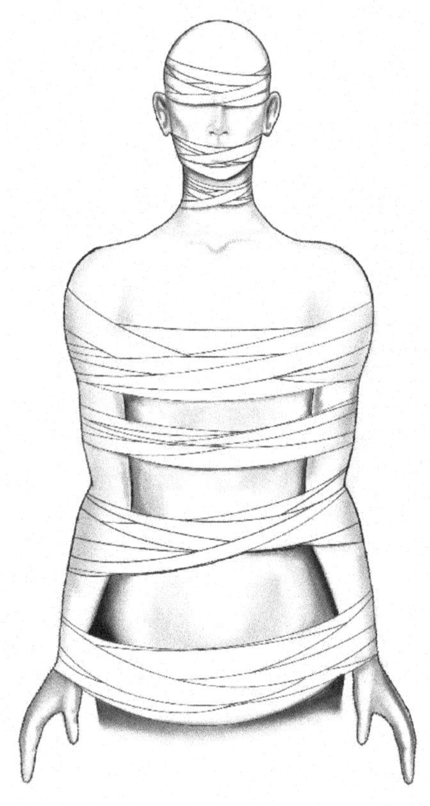

Now that you're aware of how JAMP© (AL-SAMARRAI, 2020) can work for you, we can begin our descent down the mountain. There will be moments, throughout your healing process when you trip on the staircase. You will miss a step, get that sickening feeling in the pit of your stomach, and stumble. And do you know what? That is ok. Life is a dance. You're bound to lose your footing every once in a while. You're not meant to be perfect. You're meant to be human. We're not trying to help you turn yourself into a robot that never slips up and lives a picture-perfect life. You have to remember that the rain and the summer sun are both beautiful parts of life. Accepting the rain and the trauma; seeing it as equal to the sun and the good times, is going to take you to a place of balance. In fact, start correlating thunderstorms with good days and sun with bad days. Change things up a little. Embrace everything. Breathe new meaning into your existence and learn to love yourself for everything that you are. When you can shift your mindset in this way and change the narrative, it will be that much more difficult for the "devil you know" to keep you in your uncomfortable comfort zone.

The glitch becomes like a vacuum, sucking more stories into it so that it can bury the real story far beneath the surface. It continues to project images that are not entirely related to the initial trauma so that you don't know how to stop it. This is the reason why people can spend years in therapy and feel as though they've truly turned a corner, only for their progress to be dashed away by another instance of trauma. At that point, while they haven't fallen all the way down their positive spiral, they begin recollecting their pain. This turns into a glitch-fueled cycle of thinking:

- Bad things always happen to me.

- This was bound to happen sooner or later.
- I knew I shouldn't have done (X).
- I'm never going to make it through this.
- I don't have the strength to get up this time.
- I'm just too tired.
- This is the end of the road for me.
- I am worthless.
- Nobody cares about this pain I am experiencing.

You are being terrorized by this glitch and it has led you to believe that this recent trauma is compounded by the initial trauma. You need to get rid of the devil you know.

The Devil You Know

How can you be safe and comfortable when you are being terrorized on the inside? The short answer: you can't. However, you feel that you would rather dance with the devil you know than the devil you don't. As part of the previous chapter, we looked at the archetypes that might be most dominant in you. Archetypes, in themselves, cannot be altered, but you can heal your trauma archetype so that it no longer defines you. That will then give you the leverage to take on different aspects of the archetypal characteristics.

Before you can do this, you need to heal the stories that keep you attached to the trauma on a daily basis. The problem with the human mind is that it often thinks it knows more than it actually does. We reviewed this in *Perspective vs. Prophecy*. This is part of the reason why we have reiterated several topics and defined them in further detail as we have progressed with this book. People tend to stick to what they know even if they have all of the facts to the contrary.

For instance, you might possess several characteristics of all of the archetypes that we looked at in the previous chapter, but you'll cling to the ones that you believe are the most representative of your trauma and who you are at this point in time. This is known as confirmation bias and it helps the glitch stay alive long after you think you've made your way out of it. This is why we need to reroute the energy from the complex so that the glitch can no longer survive and continue to project its images up toward you.

This bias will have you dying 100 times from the same bullet because it makes you remember and interpret things that go along with your current set of beliefs and not with actual facts.

Dying 100 Times from One Bullet

JAMP© (AL-SAMARRAI, 2020) will give you the fortitude to stop re-experiencing your trauma over and over again. The glitch hides in the moments when you think that the trauma could have destroyed you, but it didn't...but it could have...but it didn't. This back and forth makes you guarded as you try to protect yourself from an invisible terror that could come and finish you off the way it "could" have in the first place. Not only this, but it will have you diving into dark thoughts when you are at your most vulnerable. Thoughts such as:

- What did I do to make them do this to me?
- I deserved it.
- I'm such an idiot and I make people react to me in this way.

- I shouldn't have left home that day. Then I wouldn't have been in the accident that cost me my legs.
- I made the biggest mistake of my life by leaving my career for another.

Whatever the situation is which has made you live inside this glitch – whether it's trauma, death of a loved one, loss of some sort, or a rebirth that you haven't accepted – feeding confirmation biases only makes things worse. It keeps you sitting alongside the devil you know and you will feel like you deserve every bit of agony that comes your way.

Yes, pain is a part of life, but there is a difference between traumatic pain and transformative pain, in the same way that there is a difference between the pain of falling down and breaking your leg and the pain of training your muscles in the gym. They aren't the same and you need to identify which of the two you're learning to get comfortable.

Getting comfortable with transformative discomfort is necessary. Being comfortable with traumatic pain is not.

Overcoming Confirmation Bias

We all live with confirmation bias. People who suffer from trauma will confirm thoughts that are related to their trauma. People who are provided with positive beliefs and the support that they need in their fundamental years are able to confirm positivity. However, that doesn't mean that people who had a fairly normal childhood won't get caught in their own glitches at some point. There are countless war veterans who come from loving homes who can confirm this. They, just like everyone else who has been exposed to severe trauma, struggle with the glitch long after the trauma of war is over in the physical realm. Here is how you can begin overcoming a negative confirmation bias:

- Look for as many facts to the contrary as possible. If you believe that you deserved your trauma, look for facts that disprove this. It can be something as simple as using the internet to search phrases such as, "Trauma is never the victim's fault," or "All career choices are valid." The results will give you tons of information contrary to what you're thinking and feeling.
- Consult with a certified JAMP© (AL-SAMARRAI, 2020) Coach. It helps to speak with someone who can stop the echoes or confirmations from seeping into reality.

This just reaffirms why JAMP© (AL-SAMARRAI, 2020) works. It works on all aspects of trauma – from physical to mental and spiritual binds that keep you in the glitch.

*

A frog in a slow-boiling pot will never try to escape. As the water gradually heats up, it will begin to feel uncomfortable, but by the time the water is too hot, the heat will exhaust the creature and it will be too late for it to escape. Don't get comfortable with the pain of trauma. It holds you in place until it's too late – until the complex collapses.

CHAPTER 14 – CROSSING STREAMS

C*oulda, woulda, shoulda, but I didn't do that.* They aren't just popular song lyrics. They are one of the glitch's tools to keep you falling back down those first few steps of the healthy spiral. Something that we've done, as a species, is evolved our ability to think. This is both a blessing and a curse because instead of shifting away from the instinctive side of our brain and becoming more enlightened, we've become trapped in our minds. We've gone from feeling in the body, and moving on from the feeling once it has dissipated, to fueling the pain in the body – which trauma causes – with our minds. We are all overthinkers at some level. Overthinking in conjunction with trauma is a match made in glitch heaven.

As we wrap up this final chapter, we are going to be leaving you with a few short words on washing the interruptions downstream and revitalizing your energy.

Wash It Down the Stream

The glitch will interrupt your stream. It will build a dam and stop this stream of life from flowing into love, growth, creation, and progress. To wash it away, you need to stop rationalizing the trauma as something that was your fault. Stop the "if only I..." line of thinking. There is no past and there is no future. There is only this present moment. To live in your past is to live in your memory. To live in the future is to live in your imagination. Live in the present moment and you will live your real life.

In those times when you feel like you need answers to what happened to you, stop and ask yourself what will come of finding those answers. Will you have closure? Will it erase the trauma from your mental and physical memory? Will you wake up and instantly feel better, as if the trauma was just some type of bad dream?

You cannot strong-arm your way through trauma with rational thought alone, partly because the trauma itself wasn't a rational occurrence. Here are some of the ways you might be trying to rationalize and, therefore, minimize your pain and what you can do instead.

Minimization/ Rationalization	**Alternative**
My parents hit me, but at least I had parents to provide for me.	My parents hurt me and I am struggling to come to terms with that. My pain is just as valid as anyone else's.
I shouldn't be allowing this to affect me at my age.	Trauma has no age limit. I am going through the normal motions of being traumatized and I will find success with JAMP© (AL-SAMARRAI, 2020).
It's been long enough. I should be over this. This is what my mom meant when she said I blow things out of proportion.	Time does not heal all wounds; treatment does. My feelings are not infantile.
I have so much to be grateful for, so why can't I be happy? This is what my dad meant when he said I don't appreciate what he does for me.	Gratitude for the things I have cannot nullify the pain that I feel. I can be appreciative of my life and still be hurt by my trauma.

Accepting yourself as you are, even in the grips of the glitch, weakens the glitch's power over you. Beating yourself up for feeling only makes it stronger. When you have worked on your tendency to rationalize and overthink, you can begin revitalizing your energy.

Revitalizing Your Energy

Letting go of the glitch is vital to your ability to feel revitalized so that you can experience this blip that you are afforded – the blip in time called life! 100 years goes by pretty quickly. Just think of how fast your first 30, 40, 50, or 60+ years have gone by. Can you remember the joy of getting your first car as if it were yesterday? Can you recall your homecoming dance, prom, or last day of school? Can you remember moving into your first apartment?

How long ago did all of these events, which are ingrained in your memory, happen?

Trauma doesn't heal with time. All that it does is eat into the time that you have on this earth. It takes away your hope and your energy. Just like the milestones that you can so clearly remember, the next couple of years will fly by, and the next couple of years after that. You will leave these years out with little to no zest for life because your energy levels will be so low. Your body cannot live in an active stress response for prolonged periods of time. There is only so much energy to go around.

JAMP© (AL-SAMARRAI, 2020) has the power to revitalize your energy levels and give you a more hopeful approach to life.

*

You've officially made it to the end of this book and we would like to commend you for the effort that you are putting into healing your trauma. This first step is a good indication that your glitch's days are numbered. You are on a path to recovery and we would like to help you navigate that path with ease. Head over to the *Helpful Links* section for more details on how to contact us.

For those of you who selected this book to get more insight into JAMP© (AL-SAMARRAI, 2020) from a practitioner's perspective, we would like to welcome you to visit the website for JAMP© (AL-SAMARRAI, 2020) training which can also be found in the *Helpful Links* section.

IN CLOSING

Life is a beautiful, painful, messy experience. Trying to avoid discomfort is like trying to avoid breathing. It is part of everyone's journey. What makes the journey that much sweeter is being able to accept that which we cannot change and making the effort to change that which we can. Trauma is an unfortunate side-effect of being alive. Many of us have experienced trauma on some level. Even if the trauma hasn't been overt and has, rather, been covert, it can have a trickle-down effect for years to come. Due to the difficulty that our conscious mind has in processing the events that we did not understand at the time of their occurrence, these fragments are not digested by our physical, mental, or spiritual systems. As a result, our minds desperately try to make sense of the events, but because there is no sense to make of them, the events continue to play out in our responses to potential triggers. For some, when trauma has been severe enough, it will present itself in the form of imagery and dreams. For others, who have become prone to suppressing their memories, it will show up in the body. It will be a sinking feeling in the pit of your stomach. It will be the palpable energy that tingles in your lips, fingertips, posterior, and other extremities. You will hear words like "anxiety" and "mental disorder," yet you'll have very little understanding of what that means, where it all stems from, and how to treat the core problem.

What happens thereafter is that you become stuck in a loop. We call this the glitch. The glitch is the reliving of past trauma and it can take on a life of its own, giving life to the complexes that you feel define your life. And we say "feel" because, more often than not, it is not a part of your consciousness. It has splintered off from your consciousness because of your inability to accept and digest the event. Language, in itself, is a very curious thing. We hear the word accept and we automatically think that it is synonymous with condonation. You don't have to condone what happened to accept and digest it. We are not saying that trauma is good or that it is right when we say that it is a "normal" part of the human experience. Normality is subjective and it needs to be seen in the context in which the trauma occurred. As the saying goes, what is normal to the spider is chaos to the fly. Acceptance does not condone wrongdoing; it sets you free from it so that you no longer need to be prisoner a to it. This can be difficult.

This is where JAMP© (AL-SAMARRAI, 2020) comes in.

Reconnecting your body, mind, and spirit will help you process and digest the shrapnel that is embedded in the complexes which were created by the trauma. This is how you short-circuit the glitch. Becoming more mindful of your presence in the moment and steadying your body, while simultaneously releasing the rigidity in your physical form, will reduce the severity of your triggers. This will provide you with small wins. These small wins will, in turn, show you that you can respond to external and internal stimuli in a calmer and more conscious manner.

You don't have to carry generational trauma with you for the rest of your life. If you had a seemingly stable childhood and were traumatized later on by people who are external to your tribe, you don't need to identify with this trauma. If you experienced a harrowing loss – loss of limb, career, or any part of who you thought you were – it doesn't have to stop you from moving forward. We are not born to be the same person for the rest of our lives. We are not meant to live the same cycle on repeat until we leave the physical realm of existence.

If you feel that the content in this book speaks to you and your experiences, we urge you to get in touch with us. We have affordable treatments, offered by several JAMP© (AL-SAMARRAI, 2020) practitioners who can assist you. You can learn more about the principles of JAMP© (AL-SAMARRAI, 2020) in overcoming the glitch via our YouTube channel. Alternatively, navigate to our website to speak with us.

We look forward to welcoming you and to helping you move on from the glitch.

HELPFUL LINKS

1. Website - https://www.instituteforconflict.com/
2. LinkedIn (Dr. Lahab) – https://www.linkedin.com/in/dr-lahab-al-samarrai-9b3aabb/
3. Facebook - https://www.facebook.com/institute.for.conflict
4. Instagram - https://www.instagram.com/institute.for.conflict/
5. YouTube - https://www.youtube.com/channel/UC_1xmztcqFgsrhDAdOMthyA/about
6. JAMP© (AL-SAMARRAI, 2020) Training Institute - https://www.jamptraininginstitute.com/
7. JAMP© (AL-SAMARRAI, 2020) Training Institute Podcast - https://www.jamptraininginstitute.com/podcast
8. Institute For Conflict Individuation Podcast - https://www.instituteforconflict.com/podcast
9. JAMP© (AL-SAMARRAI, 2020) University https://www.jampuniversity.com
10. JAMP© (AL-SAMARRAI, 2020) Online https://www.jamponline.com

REFERENCES & CITATIONS

1. Al-Samarrai, L. (2020). Jungian Advanced Motor Processing© https://www.instituteforconflict.com/jamp-training
2. Al-Samarrai, L. (2021). *Jungian Advanced Motor Processing© (JAMP©)* (AL-SAMARRAI, 2020) *The Future of Treatment* [19 cases on its efficacy & validation to induce measurable positive change quickly the study utilities three quantitative measure the Posttraumatic Cognitions Inventor (PTCI), Somatic Symptom Scale (SSS) & Adverse Childhood Experience (ACEs).]. https://www.instituteforconflict.com/jamp-training
3. Al Samarrai, L. (2021, 1 23). *In The Time of Corona & JAMP©* (AL-SAMARRAI, 2020)*: Jung's Map Of The Soul Chapter 9*. The IFC Individuation Podcast. https://www.instituteforconflict.com/podcast/episode/ae10de0b/in-the-time-of-corona-and-jampc-jungs-map-of-the-soul-chapter-9-of-time-and-eternity-synchronicity
4. Al Samarrai, L. (2021, 04 05). *In the time of Corona & Healing*. Institute for Conflict. https://www.instituteforconflict.com/podcast/episode/30fb22e8/in-the-time-of-corona-and-healing-jungian-advanced-motor-processingc-the-future-of-trauma-treatment
5. Al-Samarrai, L. (2022) The Inception of Jungian Advanced Motor Processing (JAMP) —A 21st Century Approach to Treating Trauma. Journal of Behavioral and Brain Science, 12, 116-130. doi: 10.4236/jbbs.2022.124007.

6. Hall, James, A., 1983. Jungian Dream Interpretation; A Handbook of Theory and Practice. Toronto, Canada: Inner City Books.
7. Kalsched, Donald., 2013. Trauma and The Soul; A Psycho-Spiritual Approach Human Development and its Interruption. New York, New York: Routledge.
8. Sidoli, Mara., 2000. When the Body Speaks; The Archetypes in the Body. Philadelphia, PA: Routledge.
9. Stein, Murray., 1998. Jung's Map of the Soul; An Introduction. Chicago, Illinois: Open Court.
10. Whitmont, Edmond, C., 1993. The Alchemy of Healing; Psyche and Soma. Berkley, California: North Atlantic Books.
11. Wilmer, Harry, A., 1987. Practical Jung; Nuts and Bolts of Jungian Psychology. Asheville, North Carolina: Chiron Publication.
12. Jung, C.G., 2020. Aspects of the Feminine:(From Volumes 6, 7, 9i, 9ii, 10, 17, Collected Works) (Vol. 1). Princeton University Press.

Made in USA - Kendallville, IN
82764_9798354974429
12.13.2022 1323